P9-AQY-635

Aidan's Way

STARBUCK

Aidan's Way

The Story of a Boy's Life
and a Father's Journey

Sam Crane

SOURCEBOOKS, INC.
NAPERVILLE, ILLINOIS

Copyright © 2002 by Sam Crane
Cover design © 2002 by Sourcebooks, Inc.
Cover image credit line

All rights reserved. No part of this book may be reproduced in any form or by any electronic or mechanical means including information storage and retrieval systems—except in the case of brief quotations embodied in critical articles or reviews—without permission in writing from its publisher, Sourcebooks, Inc.

Published by Sourcebooks, Inc.
P.O. Box 4410, Naperville, Illinois 60567-4410
(630) 961-3900
FAX: (630) 961-2168
www.sourcebooks.com

Library of Congress Cataloging-in-Publication Data

Crane, Sam.
Aidan's way: the story of a boy's life and a father's journey /
Sam Crane.
cm.
ISBN 1-57071-903-9
1. Philosophy, Taoist. I. Title.
BL1920 .C73 2002
181'.114—dc21

                                        2002003137

Printed and bound in the United States of America
XX 10 9 8 7 6 5 4 3 2 1

For Aidan

Contents

Aidan's Way

Prologue

Chuang Tzu, an ancient Chinese philosopher, tells a story of a tree sheltering the village shrine:

> ...*a chestnut oak so huge thousands of oxen could gather in its shade. It measured a hundred spans around, and in height it rivaled mountains. It rose eighty feet before the branches began, and dozens of them were so large you could make them into boats. People came in droves to gaze at this tree. It was like a fair.*

One day, a master carpenter walked past it. He did not stop. His apprentice, however, was deeply impressed:

> *Since I first took up the axe in your service, master, I've never seen timber so marvelous, so full of potential. But you didn't even bother to look at it...*

The master carpenter scoffed at the lowly apprentice, pointing out all the flaws that his practiced eye could see in the massive, gnarled hulk.

It's worthless wood. If you made a boat from it, the boat would sink. If you made a coffin from it, the coffin would rot in no time. If you made tools from it, the tools would break in no time. If you made doors and gates from it, they'd sweat sticky sap. If you made pillars from it, they'd soon be full of termites. That tree has no potential whatsoever.

That night as the master carpenter slept, the tree spoke to him in his dream:

What were you comparing me to? Trees with beautiful, fine-grained wood? Fruit trees—hawthorn, pear, orange, citron? Once their fruit is ripe, they're picked clean, ransacked and plundered. Their large branches are broken down; their small limbs are scattered. It makes their lives miserable. And instead of living out the years heaven gave them, they die halfway along their journey. All that abuse of the world—they bring it upon themselves. It's like that for all things.

I've been perfecting uselessness for a long time. Now, close to death, I've finally mastered it. And it's of great use to me.

When the master carpenter mentioned this dream to the apprentice, the younger man was puzzled. Why, if the tree was determined to be useless, did it serve the village shrine so well? The master carpenter replied:

Shhh! Say no more about it! It's only resting there. If people don't have a way of understanding such a great oak, they'll rail against it. Don't you think someone would have cut it down long ago if it wasn't by the shrine? Look, it isn't like the rest of us: it's harboring something utterly different. If we praise its practicality, we'll miss the point altogether, won't we?

I.

Difficulty in the Beginning

A boy!

He was our first child: a strong, healthy boy; eight pounds, eleven ounces; high scores on his initial pediatric exams. Everything was fine.

We knew what we would name him: Aidan. We had hit upon this name two months earlier, in August, when we were walking around a favorite pond in Vermont, a pleasant late summer stroll under the pines. Maureen was drawn to one of the translations from the Gaelic she had found: Aidan—warmth of the home. That sounded right to her. This child would fill our hearts and lives, enlarge our loving and warm embrace, make us into a family.

Aidan would also break a three-generation tradition in my family. My given name is George, George Thomas. My father was George William and my grandfather, George Henry. The middle name was taken from the maternal grandfather; in my case from Thomas Aloysius Lane. It was rather eerie, because all of us Georges had birthdays within four days of one another in January, mine on the twenty-first, my father's on the twentieth, and my grandfather's on the twenty-third. But with my son, all of this would be broken. He would be born in October and he would be Aidan. This did not bother me in the least. I was not beholden to the line of George. I didn't much care for the name, in fact. More important, I would not tie my son to me or the past; he would be different, he would make his own way, as St. Aidan had, when he set out in the seventh century from his native Ireland to bring the Gospels to the pagans of Northern England.

Our Aidan came home with his mother the third day after he was born. They might have come earlier except for the cesarean delivery. The very last stages of the birth had been difficult. Aidan's head was simply too big to fit through Maureen's pelvis and eighteen hours of arduous, induced labor finally gave way, in the wee hours of the morning, to the operating room. None of this seemed ominous, however. The birth was two weeks past the due date, but we had heard that first babies were often late; and the move to a surgical resolution was welcome at the time—Maureen was beyond exhaustion. It could even be taken as a positive sign: the baby was so big and healthy that he could not squeeze through his mother's narrow hips. The initial medical observations all seemed to confirm that he was strong and sturdy. Only the happiest expectations accompanied them home.

We were ready for Aidan. His room was all made up: a newly assembled crib not far from the door, a changing table just across from it, and, against the third wall, a well-restored child's wardrobe that had belonged to Maureen's grandmother. We didn't overdo the decorations—that was not our style. A certain plainness pervaded the room. A brown rug, beige walls, and yellow curtains kept the light low and warm. There was little in the way of nursery flounce and frills; few toys or cartoon characters cluttered the scene. We had everything we needed—diapers, bassinet, black and white mobile—but we didn't need to be fancy.

The straightforwardness of the decor reflected our emotional guardedness. All through the relatively problem-free pregnancy, we held back, not wanting to invest all of our hopes in this child-to-be for fear of...of something we could not know. Maureen had only reluctantly acceded to her mother's wishes for a baby shower, and then just a month before her expected delivery date, well past the time when a miscarriage might have terminated the happy images in our minds. We were not scared, just careful. With her working background as a nurse, Maureen knew all too well how many things could go wrong medically with a pregnancy. I was slow to open up emotionally to most anything. A certain male stolidity was deeply inscribed in my personality, even if it was sometimes broken by frenetic outbursts. My father used to tell me I was born forty years old. So, I did not give my passions free rein in anticipation of a new child.

We were careful, but not pessimistic.

The birth was not a surprise for us. Quite to the contrary, we had waited to have children; waited until we were safely settled in careers, Maureen's nursing and my college teaching; waited until we had bought a house and gained our financial footing; waited until we were well past our youthful follies. Maureen was thirty-five and I, thirty-four. We would be older parents, responsible and ready; able to give our child a comfortable home and a good start. It was easy to be confident and proud. Now that the miracle of birth had happened, everything seemed possible.

And he did, indeed, warm our home. Coming back from work one afternoon, the fifth or sixth day of Aidan's life, I found him with Maureen on the glassed-in back porch of our modest house. She had dressed him in a cotton one-piece baby suit, white with large pink and brown rabbits arrayed across it. He was swathed in receiving blankets and tucked in a rustic infant carrier, woven from thick straw, that a French friend had given us. A small pillow supported his tiny head. The mid-autumn chill had given way to a temperate afternoon; yellow-white sunlight filled the room and brightened the feeling. Aidan peeked out from his refuge, narrow eyes turned up by a crinkled smile. He held his right hand up next to his head, slowly opening and closing his fist, discovering fingers and movement and shapes and smells. Maureen was radiant.

I came into the scene and was immediately relieved. My professional persona melted away in the face of familial perfection. All of my workaday cares—lectures to write, papers to grade, students to counsel, meetings to attend—fled from my mind as I sat down in the welcoming sunshine next to my son and wife. The orange and red leaves on the trees shone forth against the deepening blue sky. Aidan wrapped his tiny fist around my finger and smiled. We didn't say anything, we didn't have to say anything and, in our silence, everything was said.

A few days later, everything changed.

It was not clear what had happened at first. The outward signs were Aidan's blue lips and stilled chest. Maureen, who had turned away from him for only a minute, found him in his carrier and realized something was terribly wrong: he was not moving air, slipping into unconsciousness. She scooped him up and rapped him on the back to revive him. He came around, but the shock of the moment impelled Maureen to call the doctor, who told her to come in immediately. He seemed fine on the ride there, but then, at the doctor's office, he stopped breathing again. Just quit. After about a minute, he inhaled, the pink came back to his face, all for no apparent reason. His airway was not blocked, he was not congested, he was not making any sort of strange movements or sounds. He just stopped breathing, twice in about three quarters of an hour. The pediatrician admitted him to the hospital.

It was then that they called me. I was in class, team-teaching with another instructor, an economist friend of mine. Our topic was East Asian politics and economics, how Taiwan and South Korea had grown so rapidly in the 1960s: I did the politics and she did the economics. I could not have been farther away, intellectually, from where Maureen was at that moment. We were going back and forth, the economist and I, on some abstruse theoretical point when a knock came at the door. The twelve students at the large table all turned their heads in unison and looked to the back of the room. Before I could respond, a security guard stepped in and huskily announced:

"Professor Crane, there's a message for you to call this number right away."

He held a slip of paper in his hand. I rose and excused myself to my colleague and the class, and went out with the uniformed man. He told me that the number was for the local hospital and that my wife was looking for me, something about the baby. Upon hearing his words, my mind narrowed to the necessity of finding a telephone. I did not allow my thoughts to wander to what might be wrong but concentrated completely on the immediate task of talking to Maureen. Luckily, there was a phone right around the corner.

After one ring, a nurse answered. I told her I was looking for Maureen, who was well-known there since she worked just upstairs. My body did not move a muscle in the minute or two it took for her to pick up the receiver; I stood, head pressed against a cold brick wall, shoulder wedged into the corner of the small phone booth, and waited for her voice. And when it came, it was edgy and fast:

"Sam, something's wrong, Aidan's not breathing, he just stops and they have to give him oxygen to bring him back, and they don't know why it's happening, we may have to go to Springfield....come...now."

Her tone told me more than the words she spoke. She was clearly scared for our child. I sensed the danger and, without pressing for more details, told her I would come right away. My coat and bag were back in the classroom, however, and I would have to retrieve them first. As I reentered the room, all eyes silently followed my progress around the large rectangular seminar table and back to my place. I gathered my things and whispered to my friend that something had come up at home and I would let her know later how things were. Nodding to the students, I calmly left without a word.

The short drive to the hospital was dominated by ill-formed thoughts of what might be happening. He had stopped breathing. Did he choke on something? Had he turned his face into his pillow and almost smothered himself? But Maureen had said that it kept happening and they did not know why and that we might have to go to Springfield.

I knew well enough what Springfield meant: the large medical center there was the place that emergency cases were sent from our small-town hospital. The difficult pregnancies wound up in the neonatal unit there, the very sick babies were sent off to their intensive care unit. If they were thinking of Springfield, it must be something serious, more involved than a simple choking. As I turned these terrible thoughts over in my head, I did not feel nervous or upset. It was all too remote and unreal.

Once in the hospital, I stepped off the elevator on the third floor and found my way down the hall to the last door on the left. There, huddled around a strange device—a large metal bassinet-like contraption with a plexiglass hood over the top and several tubes running into its side—were Maureen, our pediatrician, another doctor friend of ours, a respiratory therapist, and two nurses. Aidan was lying inside the apparatus, on his right side, facing outward. A strained stillness hung in the air. The respiratory therapist was leaning over Aidan, quietly urging him on:

"C'mon baby, c'mon and breathe, you can do it darling, c'mon and breathe..."

She gently jostled him and held an oxygen mask to his nose. Maureen's face was pale and taut. The others shifted about uneasily.

It seemed that Aidan would stop breathing at regular intervals. "Apnea" is the medical term for this condition, but the word denotes a symptom, not a cause. Neither the doctor nor the therapist could determine why it was happening to him. All they could say was that it was very unusual. Infant apnea most often occurs intermittently, only once or twice a month or, at worst, a couple of times a week. Some babies stop breathing and never start again, victims of Sudden Infant Death Syndrome. Aidan was quitting every half hour or so, requiring oxygen and manual stimulation to bring him back. By the time I had arrived, it had been going on for long enough that the local doctor knew the situation was beyond the capacity of the small hospital. He said Aidan should be sent to the pediatric intensive care unit in Springfield.

Intensive care. Springfield. The day that had started out like the nine before it, with our healthy boy happily tucked in his carrier, was now descending into the most dire medical condition. I had not been in an intensive care unit for many years. My last memory of one was my grandmother's death: the intensive care unit was the place they took her to die. That's what happens in such places, and that was where Aidan was bound.

As we waited for the ambulance to arrive—it would take at least two hours for the pediatric intensivists to organize themselves and make the trip from Springfield to fetch Aidan—Maureen finally broke under the strain of it all. She is an extraordinarily strong-willed person. When faced with emergencies, she can stifle her emotions for long stretches and focus on what needs to be done, a consequence of her medical experience. But she had been doing that already for hours and the grim specter of her baby being assigned to intensive care was one burden too many. We stepped across the hall into an empty room, a waiting room of some sort, to think through our preparations for the transfer to Springfield. Maureen sat and cried, learning in the hardest way imaginable a mother's pain. Our doctor friend, the woman who would later become Aidan's godmother, sat with her. Though numb and confused, I was still standing. We would have to plan for at least a few days in Springfield, for tests and specialists and procedures. There would be papers to sign, diagnoses to consider. We would have to steel ourselves for the ordeal.

When the team from Springfield arrived the uncertainty and anxiety of the moment lifted. They were confident and calm, seemingly omniscient. They knew precisely what they were doing. What for our little hospital was an unprecedented emergency, was for them just another day's work.

A tall, stocky black man was their leader. A resident physician from the big medical center, he crisply issued commands to his respiratory therapist and intensive care nurse. They very quickly summed up the situation and decided that they would have to intubate Aidan for the long ride back to their unit. This would require inserting a tube into his lungs to make sure they could maintain a steady stream of vital oxygen. The local pediatrician told me not to watch, but I had to. I saw several adults circle around Aidan, holding him in place and forcing a small, curved plastic nozzle into his mouth and down his throat. He fought valiantly, spitting the ghastly object back at them four times. Their size and strength and expertise finally outdid him, however. As they released their grip on him, his sobs slowly subsided. An oxygen tank hissed quietly.

Maureen and I could not ride with them to Springfield but would have to go by ourselves. They told us not to rush, not to try to keep up with the ambulance. We had to go home anyway, to pick up some things—clothes, toothbrushes, documents—for a few days in the hospital. Once we were on the highway, eastbound to Springfield, the dark of the night pressed in around us, blurred by a steady rain. We did not talk much, each of us lost in the cascade of misfortune. An uncontrollable grief rose up from deep inside me and spilled out of my eyes in salty tears. I did not call out, I did not sob, but just cried silent streams of sadness and fear. Aidan was out there in the darkness ahead of us, leading us on to somewhere we had never been, a place we could not imagine.

We were supposed to go back to Asia. That was the plan. I had arranged for a year away from my usual teaching duties, time to study and write about Asian politics, my academic specialty. Maureen and Aidan and I were to travel to Australia the next fall. Aidan would have his first birthday in Canberra while I ran a seminar at the Australian National University. In the spring, we would all go to Kyoto, Japan, where I would teach and write. Perhaps Aidan would utter his first words while we strolled amid the cherry blossoms in the old imperial gardens. He would start out in cosmopolitan fashion, a world traveler before he was two. It was so very different from my conventional suburban upbringing, and I was captivated by the prospect of shaping my son's life in this way.

Only recently had I started to believe that I could really control such things. For most of my life, until just a year or two before Aidan was born, I had doubted my ability to plan and guide the course of my life. Perhaps it was my father's old Irish fatalism that he shouted to the world when the drink drowned him in turbulent self-pity; or maybe it was the hippie skepticism of the times, the studied non-competitiveness of certain longhaired youth. Whatever it was, in high school, as my peers crafted perfect résumés, with high grades and happy activities designed to guarantee Ivy League admission, I hung around with a slovenly crew, unconcerned with what the future might hold. The modest state university nearby worked just fine for me, and when the time came to fashion some sort of career strategy, I evaded the workaday world and backed into graduate school. I did not have a clear vision of becoming a college professor, but simply followed where the opportunities led.

One thing had captured my imagination in college: China. At my small school, there were only two full-fledged classes offered—one in philosophy and one in sociology—but having taken them, I wanted to learn more. Modern Chinese politics became my primary interest, but I could sit for hours reading through the grand narratives of Chinese history and reflecting upon the deep traditions of Chinese thought. So, it seemed quite natural that I should study the language and keep reading about Chairman Mao's tragic escapades and, some day, find my way to the Great Wall. That's what I did in graduate school, that and a lot of other social science stuff that just seemed to get in the way of my learning about China.

But when I finally had the chance to go there, to live for ten months and study and move through a wholly different culture and speak to people in their language—however rough my Chinese—it had a transformative effect on me. I began to shed my doubt. It seemed like I could take charge of what I was doing. I could cast myself into the massive crowds of Beijing or Shanghai or Guangzhou and find my way around to precisely the restaurant or park or anything else I wanted. Maureen noticed the change when she came to visit for a month and we traveled up and down the country on our own. She could see a new purposefulness in my personality and she told me so. I felt it too: a new sense of efficacy.

My return to the U.S. brought me back to an intractable reality. I had to find a job in a flat academic market. My prospects were not very good. The placement office in my department sent my file to thirty or forty different colleges and universities, many places I dreaded. Only one good school sent a follow-up, asking me for samples of my writing. But as the months went by and that came to naught and nothing else seemed to be happening, I fell back into my earlier and deeper uncertainty. My fate was out of my control, tossed on the whims of the job market, and I just had to go along for the ride.

One day, a call came and that led to an interview and, finally, a job. It was a good position at a high profile university in Washington, D.C., not a bad place to keep track of China. But I had no choice: it was that job or no job and another depressing year of being a little-too-old-for-this graduate student. I accepted the offer, of course, and we were fairly happy. Maureen finished her nursing degree and I discovered I could teach eager twenty-year-olds about

Chinese politics and international relations. Yet for all of the opportunities we had before us, we felt confined, like we had been compelled to move into the sprawling megalopolis of northern Virginia, without due consideration of what we really wanted in life. We were being swept along frenetic career paths, but were increasingly unsure of where they led. We needed a choice.

The confidence I had gained on my first trip to China had not completely worn away, and I planned a search for another job. We would concentrate on smaller schools in the Northeast, those leafy liberal arts colleges where the pay was good and the institutional scale smaller. I applied to three of four and, surprisingly, was given an interview at one.

Everything went very well. I was comfortable and self-assured, knowing that if this chance fell through I still had my Washington perch. They offered me the job. It was an ironic turnaround: so many of my high school peers yearned to attend this sort of elite college and now I, who cared less then, would someday be teaching their children at the school of their dreams. And then things took an even more fortuitous turn. Just after I accepted the new job, another well-known university called and asked if I would like to teach for a year in China! With this, it seemed my professional life was set. Maureen and I would go to China for a year and upon our return take up the new job in Massachusetts, an initial three-year appointment with a strong chance for more permanent tenure beyond. Never before had I ever mastered time and circumstances so completely.

It was a great year in China. We had many adventures and returned energized and happy. We had saved enough money to put a down payment on a house shortly after I settled into the new job. Maureen took a position at the local hospital, the kind of frontline nursing she was looking for. We got a dog from the pound, a spry and loyal Labrador. Everything seemed to be falling into place: we were becoming responsible adults in ways, just a year or two before, we had not quite thought possible—new jobs, new house, new dog. We were certainly ready to take the next step and confidently start a family. We could provide loving security and stability for our baby. We would take him or her on our next trip to Asia, to Australia, and Japan. And if it was a son, he would be Aidan and bring warmth to our home.

The lights were dim in the Pediatric Intensive Care Unit—PICU to those in the know—when we arrived after Aidan. It was about ten o'clock at night. The large, open ward had four beds, two to the right, two to the left. One wall was glass from floor to ceiling, so that the nurses and doctors stationed at a counter just across the hall could see everything. Aidan was in a shiny steel crib in the back left corner of the unit, his nurse standing next to him, jotting notes on her chart.

Disoriented by the long drive in the dark and the unfamiliar hospital, we quietly went over to him. He was surrounded by tubes and wires and monitors and machinery. The ventilator was still attached, a thick blue accordion-like hose running up the side of his bed right to his neck, where it narrowed down into a smooth clear plastic tube that ran into his mouth. An intravenous line was poked into his wrist. Heart and breathing monitors were taped to his chest with thin wires running from them up and back into a gaggle of gadgets looming all around the small crib. In the middle of all of this, he was asleep, his tiny chest rising and falling with reassuring regularity.

The nurse put down her notes and introduced herself. She told us that the doctors had determined that Aidan was having seizures. On the ride in the ambulance they had noticed that just before he would stop breathing, he turned his head to the right, fixed his eyes in an unblinking stare and stuck the tip of his tongue out of his mouth. This was a "subtle seizure," she said. They had given him phenobarbital, an anticonvulsant drug, and that seemed to stop the episodes. We asked her what might have caused the seizures and she said they did not know. I noticed she had irreverently long fingernails, painted a comical blue and silver, no doubt a hit with her pediatric patients.

We sat in the uncomfortable metal chairs next to Aidan's crib. The PICU was still but not silent. The beeps and boops of the various machines danced in the air, sometimes coming together in a strange rhythm, but more often fighting against one another in a constant, low-toned dissonance. Maureen stretched her hand through the tangle of tubes and wires and stroked Aidan's arm. He was flat on his back, head lolled to the right, the wisps of golden hair on his head mussed from untold hands moving him about. We sat silently, trying to understand what "subtle seizures" were. They sounded benign to me. Subtle was not ferocious, it was not pernicious; it was gentle and easy. Maybe whatever was going on was some freakish occurrence that, in the end, would pass subtly without terrible repercussions.

The resident physician, who had overseen Aidan's transport to Springfield, came in to talk to us. It was pushing midnight, but he was still clear-eyed and articulate. Confirming what the nurse had told us about the ambulance ride, he said that Aidan had been felled by seizures that interrupted his breathing. The underlying cause was not evident. He asked us if Aidan had recently had a high fever or any other unusual medical problems. We said no, everything had seemed fine. He said that a series of tests would have to be run to check for various possible causes: encephalitis, meningitis, neurological disorders. It would be a long and anxious day, maybe two days, and, he said, we should try to get some sleep.

There were no beds for parents available in the PICU. The nurse told us that they could arrange for a room at the Ronald MacDonald house just outside the entrance of the hospital. We decided that one of us should go there while the other stayed nearby. I prevailed upon Maureen to go, arguing that she would need to be fresh and sharp in the morning when the doctors started coming around and ordering tests. She hesitated, but with the nurse reassuring her that the close supervision of the PICU would guarantee Aidan's safety, she finally accepted the idea and set off. I found my way down the hall about one hundred feet and into an uninviting lounge. Alone, I did my best to darken the room but the large windows looking out on the hallway made it impossible to keep out the glaring hospital fluorescence. A stiff couch offered the best chance of sleep. I stretched myself out, closed my eyes, and found no dreams in the shallow unconsciousness that settled upon me.

Maureen was already back in the PICU by the time I awoke. She was ready to do battle, to parry any doctor's order she did not like. Aidan was stirring, coming out of the drug-induced sleep that had overwhelmed him the night before. Although he was groggy, they let us hold him. Scooping him up in her arms, and mindful of the wires and tubes still attached to him, Maureen settled him into her lap. His narrow eyes did not meet hers—he had yet to focus on worldly objects—but his thin, straight lips curled up a bit, or so it seemed.

Doctors started to come around and introduce themselves. The chief pediatric intensivist was a tall man with broad shoulders and a scraggly ponytail hanging over his collar. This was clearly his domain: other physicians and nurses deferred to him, reported to him, made way for him. When conversing with his staff, his eyes would sometimes draw to a squint and, as he took in bad news and decided what to do, his face would harden in determination: He had no doubt seen many children die and his countenance carried that heavy burden. But just as quickly as that steeliness could set upon his features, it could dissolve into a roguish good humor. Joking with comrades, finding whatever fun there might be in an intensive care unit, was likely how he survived his difficult, enthralling job. At one point that first morning, he came over and we exchanged the usual pleasantries and reviewed what little was known of Aidan's condition. Seizures, now apparently controlled by drugs, with no other obvious complications in an eleven-day-old infant, did not frighten this man. Before turning to leave he stared into my eyes and said, without hesitation or embellishment, "He'll be all right." I didn't know if his "all right" was the same as mine, but I felt then that we wouldn't lose Aidan in the PICU.

Not long afterward, Dr. Graham, a pediatric neurologist, stopped by. He was a gentle man, without the gruffness of the PICU chief. Although his job daily brought him into the lives of children with malformed or malfunctioning brains, he did not appear hardened by the toil. With a small, old-fashioned black doctor's bag by his side, he listened intently to everything we had to say, nodding unconsciously as Maureen repeated the story of her pregnancy, delivery, and Aidan's uneventful first nine days. His visit was short; no doubt he was needed by other families facing similar crises. He described various tests—a CAT scan, blood samples—and took his leave.

As the day wore on, the sense of danger abated. The PICU was becoming familiar to Maureen and me. We took turns getting lunch and wandering about the hallways around the unit. I cased the floor, eyeing where the blankets and towels were stored should we need something later. Maureen kept close track of the doctors and specialists, her nurse sensibilities merging with her motherly instincts—a formidable combination. We chatted with the nurses, who were expert at easing parental fears.

Graham returned in the afternoon. He reported that most everything appeared normal. There was no bleeding or swelling or growths of any kind. Most of the more common causes of infantile seizures were ruled out. But the CAT scan had revealed an anomaly. It seemed that the bridging structure that connected the right and left sides of the brain—the corpus callosum—was either attenuated or absent altogether. The information was not completely reliable, Graham cautioned, and further tests would have to be run: an MRI, to gain a more detailed picture of Aidan's brain. At this point, the doctor could only guess that some sort of physical malformation might have caused the seizures.

A brain defect? My mind flashed with images of permanent disability, mental retardation…

Before we could fully absorb all of what he was saying, Graham reassured us that the situation might not be as bad as it sounded. Some people lived completely normal lives without a fully developed corpus callosum; they did not have persistent seizure conditions, and their physical and mental health was fine. In any event, all of this was speculative since a more confident diagnosis required the MRI and, perhaps, other tests beyond that. As he spoke, his face remained calm and relaxed, his voice was even and unhurried; he did not project any sense of peril.

Maureen and I, unwilling to even begin to think terrible thoughts about our baby boy, embraced the optimism made available by Graham's words. It was too soon to tell whether there was a problem with the corpus callosum; and even if there were something unusual there, it did not necessarily mean a terrible prognosis. It was possible that Aidan would be fine; we would get through this awful moment and back to our happy family life in a few days. We would resume where was had left off before being so rudely interrupted by a rough and isolated bout of seizures. We would leave the PICU behind: the long-nailed nurse; the beeping machines, the friendly neurologist, and the dire threat to all of our dreams.

Years earlier, on my first trip to China, I took a boat ride on the Huangpu River, embarking from the Shanghai waterfront. It was a gray December day and a cold, wet wind knifed across the wide expanse of muddy water, cutting through clothes and skin with bone-chilling effect. The large excursion boat was loaded with sightseers, mostly Chinese people from other parts of the country come to see the big city. I ventured on deck for a short time, my coarse wool scarf cinched snugly around my neck and my furry People's Army hat pulled down over my ears. But even with that protection, the icy gusts drove me back into the large main cabin, warmed by dozens of happy day-trippers.

As I sipped a tepid cup of stale coffee and gazed out the large windows at the passing industrial cityscape, my eyes fell on the few hearty souls who stayed on the foredeck braving the freezing dampness. One man in particular commanded my attention. He was short and stocky with a ruddy complexion. Wearing only a thin cotton jacket, with no hat and no gloves, he stood motionless, head-on into the cold gusts; impassive; unaffected by the winter winds. I watched him for some time, impressed by his fortitude. I imagined him as a peasant on holiday in Shanghai, a man whose life demanded a great deal of hard work and repaid little in material comfort. He had come through bad harvests and meager provisions, had survived various political movements and injustices. The cold did not bother him; it was just another of the myriad discomforts he had to bear. I wondered if I could do it, if I could stand there, face into the wind and not let it get to me, if I could live his life. I figured then that I couldn't.

In the womb, brain development starts about three weeks after conception. The top layer of the embryo, little more than a plate of cells, begins to turn back on itself, creating the neural tube. The entire nervous system slowly takes shape as one end of the neural tube expands out to become the brain and the other elongates into the spinal cord. The brain gradually divides into three and then five sacs, or vesicles, that come to form distinct brain regions. If something goes wrong at this stage, it can be fatal: anencephaly, in which a significant portion of the brain is absent, usually results in stillbirth or death in two or three days. Other malformations at this very early stage of brain development most often produce severe mental and physical disabilities.

Aidan's brain grew normally in the first few gestational weeks, but as more complex tissues and structures started to form, something went wrong.

After about four months, neurons migrate from the neural tube to areas that will become the cerebellum, the cerebral cortex, and other important components. The brain starts to take on its characteristic appearance: two moist hemispheres of tightly folded matter gently rounded to the contours of the skull. The bridging structure that connects the two sides of the cortex, the corpus callosum, also forms at this time. However, neurons do not migrate properly, if they fail to find their precise places within the intricate neurological architecture, a number of developmental disorders are possible. The folds of the cortex may grow too large (pachygyri) or too small (polymicrogyria). There may be no folds whatsoever, leaving the brain with an eerie smoothness (lissencephaly). The link between the two hemispheres (corpus callosum) may not develop (agenesis). Most of these anomalies, except for agenesis of the corpus callosum, are associated with seizures, significant mental retardation, and other developmental delays.

It seems clear that at about four or five fetal months something interfered with Aidan's neuronal migration. The folds of his cortex grew smaller and more numerous than usual; and his corpus callosum did not come together. While all brains are unique in detail, his was truly extraordinary. It was not so much damaged—a word often used to describe such differences—as it was unusual; his brain did not break but simply grew in a singular fashion. There was no name for the form of his brain, no known syndrome to categorize it and compare it to others. It was utterly unconventional.

Aidan's brain continued to grow and develop, his neurons proliferated, migrated and matured. Many of his brain regions developed normally. By the time he was born, the size of his brain was typical; he could hear and smell and feel our touch. As with all infants, synapses, the billions of connections between brain cells, were explosively increasing in number. But Aidan's brain would diverge from the norm in one other important way during the transition from gestation to birth. The insulation of nerve processes, the myelin sheaths that help to route brain activity into regular and efficient pathways, was growing more slowly and unevenly than expected. This dysmyelination had been detected in the first MRI and it suggested that Aidan's brain might take longer to process certain types of information and to issue some electrochemical commands to his body.

I was not there when Graham explained all of this to Maureen.

It was two days after our initial arrival in the PICU and Aidan had stabilized enough to be moved out of intensive care and onto a regular hospital floor. We had taken this as a good sign: Aidan was not in immediate danger; the seizures had not returned; he was getting better. So, before we learned what the MRI had found, we decided that I should go home. Maureen's parents were due at our house and we had not yet told them, or anyone else, what had happened. It would be better for one of us to speak to them face to face, and I took on that task.

I was at home with my in-laws, having broken to them the bad news that their first grandchild was in a hospital in Springfield, when I called Maureen. Her voice cracked into sobs as soon as she knew it was me on the line. She had just spoken to Graham and he was much less optimistic. The MRI clearly showed that Aidan's corpus callosum was missing. "Agenesis of the corpus callosum," Graham had intoned. Agenesis: literally, *without birth*. My mind wrapped around that word—*agenesis*—and it was impossible to conjure up the image of a normal life that seemed plausible when Graham had first broached the issue. As Maureen caught her breath, she said other problems had been found: polymicrogyria, more and smaller folds of the cortex, and dysmyelination. Her cries rang in my ear through the impersonal telephone.

I tried to find some words to soothe her, something to say to pull us closer together at that moment our world was falling apart around us. But I could only mumble something about how we would get through it somehow, that he would be all right. I told her I would be there in the morning and hung up, head swimming with questions about how a child's brain develops and what Graham's report might mean for Aidan and us.

I was there in the morning, and we brought Aidan home the next day. The doctors were confident that the seizures were under control and there was nothing to do about the brain malformations except wait and see. It would take some months before a diagnosis could be confirmed. Graham could not predict with any confidence the extent of disability this peculiar combination of abnormalities might produce. All would depend on how Aidan developed, how his brain grew. The doctor could say, however, that there was no available research on the effects of agenesis of the corpus callosum *and* polymicrogyria *and* dysmyelination. Each had likely ramifications on its own, but the coincidence of all three together was vanishingly rare. All was further obscured by the remote possibility that some of the problems might, with some luck, prove to be less dire as Aidan matured. What looked like an overabundance of undersized folds in the brain could transform, as his brain expanded, into something closer to normal, though normality itself was most likely impossible. Or it could be an extremely unusual condition, incapacitating and untreatable. Graham was not optimistic, but neither could he be absolutely sure.

So we returned to our home with our firstborn son and waited, waited for the cold uncertainty to lift, waited for the warmth to return.

2.

The Abyss

The holidays came, as they always did. There was snow for Christmas, and icicles and puffs of frozen breath. The town was smothered and smoothed with winter, lit by thousands of tiny twinkling lights, all very small-town, handsome-white-church New England. A tree sprouted in our living room, festooned with an assortment of decorations: round glass balls, slender silken Chinese ladies, small wooden figurines, an angel on top. Cards from friends and relations were taped over the wide portal opening into the dining room. A large, impossibly red poinsettia held forth on a side table. All of our usual holiday trappings, a riot of Yuletide kitsch, lent a certain comfort and warmth to the house.

Aidan's white wicker bassinet blended perfectly into the scene, a little cloud hovering amid the cozy snowbound landscape. He rested there peacefully, his soft and rounded features swaddled in blankets, a first son tucked in a modern manger on wheels. The winter light refracted off his smooth face, adding to the hopefulness of the season. Just over two months old, he radiated newborn beauty. We decorated his little crib with a small red stocking, a black-hatted snowman, a sprig of holly. It was just enough to obscure the gray cord running out from under the covers to the apnea monitor perched nearby.

In spite of the happy season, we were awash in uncertainty, unable to know Aidan's prospects, struggling to find ways of managing our fears and anxieties. His pleasant demeanor and graceful appearance gave us some hope. He did not look abnormal or malformed. His wavy brown hair framed a gentle, symmetrical face: almond-oval eyes with thick lashes evenly set over a low-bridged nose; round cheeks sloping down to neatly curlicued lips, neither too thin nor too thick; fair, smooth skin. He was free of the bodily contortions suffered by some people with severe physical disabilities. There was no spasticity to twist his limbs akimbo, no outward physical sign that there was any significant difference here. He did not come down with colds or ear infections or any of the usual baby illnesses. How could he possibly be disabled when he cast such a happy and healthy image?

Maybe the doctors were wrong; maybe they were being too pessimistic. The physical therapist who came to the house to exercise Aidan, stretching his limbs and enlivening his body, used words like "developmental delay." This had an oddly comforting effect on me. "Delay" implied a temporary pause, a gap that, with some effort and luck, might be closed. If he was simply delayed in his development, maybe he could catch up later. Maybe, by the time he was a full year old, he would be back within a normal range of physical and mental capabilities. Perhaps it would take a little longer, but still, he might get past his delay. Such was our Christmastime wish.

It was hard to sustain hope, however, as we were daily reminded that he was not holding his head upright, he was not reaching for objects, he was not turning and rolling on the floor. When we took him to the bustling mall, filled with busy holiday shoppers, we were confronted with dozens of difficult comparisons. Over there was an infant, just a bit older than Aidan, sitting on Santa's lap, eyes wide with fascination for the splurge of red and white, then crying at the strangeness of it all, holding up a tiny hand to ward off the giant jolly alien. And here was another child, a toddler, alert and engaged with the crowded commotion surrounding her, sitting upright in her carriage, squealing happily in her own private language. Aidan, by contrast, did not focus on the thousands of images speeding past his eyes, he did not attempt to rouse himself from the comfortable recline of his carrier. He often dozed off, overwhelmed by the phenobarbital coursing through his veins.

People would approach us, attracted by our beautiful baby boy and buoyed by the merry energy of the season. "Oh...he's so cute. Is he sleepy?" How could we answer? If we said, "No, he's snowed by powerful anticonvulsant drugs," what would that do to the moment? The happy Christmas spirit would be chased away, the pall of winter solstice, the longest night of the year, would descend. Instead, we would lie, conceal the difficult truth, keep up appearances: "Yes, he's sleepy."

We concealed much in those early months. Aware of the ways that representations can harden into identities—Aidan, the Disabled Boy—Maureen and I did not invite people into our trouble and did not divulge too much of what the doctors were telling us. It was hard enough fending off expressions of pity, awkward combinations of affection and alienation. People who knew us offered sympathy for the child who might be unwhole, incomplete. They could guess at our pain, the dreams dashed, and they wanted to reassure and support. Although most often unspoken, "we're sorry," or, "we feel so bad for you," infused every syllable, every gesture. The intended kindness brought with it an uncomfortable classification: Aidan was of the pitiable, those who must be mourned; his difference required consolation. He was thus categorized, separated from some unspecified sense of normality. To avoid this estrangement, we did not reveal the emerging extent of his "delay."

Our local pediatrician was sensitive to this issue. During a routine appointment after Aidan's harrowing passage through the PICU, he asked us, "What are you telling people?" He did not assume that we would simply report to all and sundry that our boy faced potential limitations, perhaps of great profundity. And he was right. We did not want his medical condition to define him as a person. We did not want society's first impression of him to be "handicapped," or "crippled," or "abnormal." There were enough obstacles to asserting oneself in the world and we did not want to place any more in front of Aidan.

It was, then, a lonely holiday season. We had each other, Maureen and I, though it was difficult to console one another while we were hoping upon hope that he would perk up developmentally. When she broke down, overcome by the terrible possibilities, I sometimes felt resentful, as if I had to maintain all of the optimism and hold up the sky for both of us. I was not up to this task and chafed at her grief. Conversely, when I was gloomy, I did not want to bring my sorrow to her, for fear of dimming whatever brightness she might have had. So, we kept to our familiar holiday routines—making cookies, reading "A Child's Christmas in Wales," eating Chinese take-out on New Year's Eve—and held on to the promise of a newborn son.

Although all the neurons that a person's brain will ever have are present at birth, and basic brain structures are in place, cells continue to migrate from deep inside the brain to the cerebral cortex and the cerebellum for some months after birth. And neurons continue to grow and expand for years. More dramatic than these subtle changes in brain hardware after birth, however, are the transformations of brain software. The connections between neurons, or synapses, the "wiring" for many senses and functions, develop explosively in the first year of life. At birth, there are about fifty trillion synapses, a basic template for rudimentary actions and reflexes, but their number increases approximately twenty times to near one thousand trillion synapses by a child's first birthday. Vision, hearing, language, thought, and many other human capacities are shaped by this early synaptic development. Indeed, brain growth is a dynamically interactive process: external stimuli—hearing voices, seeing colors, feeling textures—play a critical role in producing fully capable and intelligent children.

Early brain development is so dynamic that profound structural abnormalities may be offset by the creation of new synaptic pathways. Brains can find ways of working even when they are physically distorted. A six-year-old girl with intractable seizures had the entire right side of her cortex surgically removed, immediately paralyzing the left side of her body and raising serious questions about her future abilities in music, math, and art, higher functions associated with the right brain. After years of therapy and education, however, she did very well in a regular middle school and could move almost all of the left side of her body. Her brain, after a radical physical change, used what tissue was left to reinvent normalcy.

Of course, certain congenital brain malformations are very often associated with disability. A child with polymicrogyria usually faces moderate to severe neurological impairment; mental retardation of some sort is widely reported. But there is always some uncertainty, and therefore hope, due to the marvelous plasticity and adaptability of young brains. Might some intensive therapy encourage synaptic compensation so that the negative effects are limited? The variability of outcomes is seen clearly in cases of agenesis of the corpus callosum (ACC). Many people function quite normally without the bridging tissue between cerebral hemispheres. In fact, cutting the corpus callosum is a surgical treatment for persistent generalized seizures. Depriving seizures of the bridge from one side of the brain to the other can limit their severity without disabling the individual. In some instances, however, the absence of the corpus callosum can lead to physical or mental deficits. Perhaps the most remarkable case is that of a young man whose moderate metal retardation is believed to be related to his ACC; but he has adapted in such a way that the autonomy of the two sides of his brain allows him to read and understand two pages of a book simultaneously.

What would be possible for Aidan's brain? Given the potential for development and change, no one could know, after only a few months, just how extensive his limitations might be. So why not flood him with stimulation of all kinds: physical, visual, aural, olfactory, whatever? Why not present that rare brain with as much information as possible, so that even if some did not take, enough would to make the most of his potential? What we needed was someone to help us engage Aidan, to animate his neurons and synapses to make them expand and thrive.

That help first arrived in the person of Linda. A physical therapist, she was sent to our house by Early Intervention, a social services agency for families with "at risk" children under three years of age. She was a pleasant person, with a calm disposition and an easy smile. Her work brought her into tense and difficult family situations several times a day, five days a week. Our confusion and anxiety were nothing new to her; she seemed to know just what to do. She handled the stress with an unusual poise, never racing her motions or raising her voice.

Placing Aidan on a blanket on the floor, she gently stretched his arms and legs. Her hands guided his, up over his head and then out, fan-like, down to his sides. She took hold of his fingers and sought his attention with smiles and clucks. Taking his legs, she curled them up at the knee in a bicycling motion, sometimes alternating one to the other, sometimes running them together. Next, she rolled him on his right side and ran her finger down his spine, trying to get him to extend and, eventually, roll onto his back. She did the same on his left side. When that was done, she eased him on to his stomach and tucked his arms under his shoulders, his hands under his chin, to encourage him to lift his head. She had dozens of ideas and tricks to stimulate the most basic movements, actions that would build into developmental milestones. To get him to lift his head, she placed a mirror in front of him, hoping that the sight of the "other" baby would draw his attention. To heighten his physical awareness, she showed us how to cradle him in our arms, his knees drawn up and his arms drawn in. We learned about "proprioception," the body's sense of itself in space; and to stimulate his, we flew him around the room like an airplane and tossed him gently up, tingling the receptors in his muscles. Linda saw that we had the usual collection of high-contrast, black and white pictures to engage his vision, and to this she added lights and colors, a dazzling array of optical delights.

Aidan, however, hardly responded. His muscle tone remained very weak, a condition known as "hypotonia," and he could raise his head only with the greatest effort. A certain limpness suffused his entire body. He could wave his arms about and kick his legs, but his movements were tentative and uncoordinated, lacking the vigor and sharpness of typical children. He was not fixing and following his vision on the various objects we presented to him, nor was he reaching for them. And he fell further and further behind the developmental schedules in the baby books. His lack of progress did not worry Linda, at least not outwardly. She kept at it, and kept us at it, never betraying a hint of despair, persevering in her positive and constructive manner.

Yet, however competent and even-tempered Linda may have been, her presence was, at first, deeply disconcerting for Maureen. Her people were from Brooklyn and suspicious of outsiders; they did not readily admit weakness or dependence. Although Maureen was not as clannish as most in her large, blue-collar, Irish-Catholic family, she had enough of their outlook to feel uneasy with the intrusion of a stranger, even one so well-intentioned. Certain things were just not discussed with others, especially something like a disability. What made it worse was that we needed Linda's help with our most intimate responsibility, caring for our child, the very thing, above all else, that we should do for ourselves. But Maureen's recognition of Aidan's need trumped her inherited mistrust and, as Linda visited more regularly, the comfort level increased.

One day, after an hour of working with Aidan, Linda was getting ready to leave and Maureen opened up to her. All of the terrible worries about Aidan's future—would he walk? talk? run?—came pouring out, all of the fears about society's response.

"People will stare, won't they?" she asked.

Linda's eyes dilated with sympathy.

"They'll rush to judge him, reduce him to some inferior status." Maureen was sobbing now. "That's what they'll do, won't they?" she insisted.

Linda stood in the doorway, the blackness of her skin in sharp contrast to the snowy winter walkway behind her. She looked into Maureen's eyes and, with the weight of three hundred and fifty years of African-America, slowly nodded her head. "Yes. That is what they will do."

Dr. Graham had maintained a certain optimism for several months. The seizures had subsided for some time, a good sign in the doctor's eyes. He noticed the obvious manifestations of Aidan's developmental delay—no fixing and following with his eyes, low muscle tone, no reaching for objects— but Graham had held open a chance for improvement. "I think it is a bit early to say whether these abnormalities are definite or not," he wrote in one follow-up letter. In the ears of two hopeful parents, searching for whatever positive possibilities there might be, this sounded rather good. It gave us something to hold onto, a thin reed to grasp, a future. If it was too early to tell, maybe there was still a chance that things would not be too bad.

April, however, lived up to its cruel reputation. It was then that Graham changed his assessment and came down clearly and unequivocally with a devastating pronouncement. Maureen and I were sitting in his austere examination room, just after an EEG that told us the seizures were returning in an especially virulent form. Aidan slept peacefully in his carriage, his six-month-old smallness wrapped in a blanket, undisturbed, for this moment, by the electrical storm in his brain. Graham's eyes focused straight at us, his facial expression sad but matter-of-fact. He had reviewed all the medical data, consulted with colleagues, and reflected upon his twenty years of experience. It was now evident to him that Aidan was not going to get better. He told us in an even, quiet voice that severe disability was certain; profound mental retardation and blindness probable; early death most likely. No more detailed prognosis was possible at this point: he could not say exactly how bad off Aidan would be or when precisely he might die. I sensed, nevertheless, he was thinking that we would be lucky if Aidan made it to his fifth birthday.

Maureen reacted powerfully and immediately. "Do you know what this means?" Her anger spilled out. "Do you know what you're doing to us?"

Graham nodded his head slightly; he knew all too well what it meant. He had, no doubt, said such things to new parents many times before and was careful with his words. After a long moment of awkward silence, he quietly spoke through tight lips with upraised eyebrows.

"Nature is cruel," he said.

It was everything any parent fears most: a newborn condemned to abnormality; a child slipping away. We wanted a happy and full life for Aidan, but that now seemed impossible. What would his life be? How could it be meaningful without mental acuity, without sight, without physical ability? The many social implications of Graham's prognosis— the alienation, the discomfort, the injustice—flitted at the margins of my mind but hardly intruded upon the central, overwhelming fact that my son was doomed to a fate I could barely imagine but that appeared perilous and depressing.

I sat silently. No words came, no tears fell. I could feel the size of the room; it was larger and emptier than it had been before, or perhaps I was just smaller and more compact. My lips tensed together as my eyes shifted from Graham to Maureen and back. I could almost see the scene zooming back, the lens opening to a wider angle with me perched above and behind myself, looking back down at the action, removed but at the same time engaged. It was, at once, unreal yet close at hand. The initial seizure crisis had been more shocking to me; it was completely unexpected and I was, then, wholly in the moment emotionally. Now, six months later, I was almost prepared for the bad news. I had had time to contemplate the worst and, even though I may have denied it, when it was put before me, I could almost take myself out of the picture. Almost. As I inhaled in preparation to speak, the focus narrowed again, the light seemed to dim and yellow, Graham's face loomed larger before me.

"What should we do?" I asked calmly.

Asking a question helped; it gave me something to deflect the full force of the doctor's words. I could turn the emotional momentum away from myself, back toward Graham. This was instinctual protection. I was shielding myself not just from the ramifications of the prognosis, but also from my own fatherly love for Aidan. If I let the doctor's words through to my heart, it would explode; I would be toppled by the harsh reality that my infant son was disabled and might die at any time. Though always careful with my affections, wary of opening myself to hurt, I was discovering that my connection to Aidan was visceral. He moved me in ways very few others could. In the six short months of his life, I had responded to his vulnerability, provided for his needs—his food, his home, his safety— and this made me vulnerable in ways I had never been before. The prospect of his demise was simply too much for me to contemplate; I needed the distraction of questioning Graham.

I listened intently to his response, carefully following every syllable. He took the question in a medically literal way and said that we should continue the seizure medication and talk to other neurologists and consult with genetic counselors if we were planning other pregnancies. I was rapt by his specificity. Each concrete suggestion was another brick in the wall I was building against the surge of emotions inside me, each task a diversion to take me away from the immediate crisis.

Of course, my question had broader implications. What should we do to make the best life possible for Aidan, however long that might be? What should we do for ourselves to survive in this maelstrom? Graham had no answers for such queries; he would not venture beyond the confines of medicine into the realm of life at large. Yet the bigger concerns would prove to be the strongest challenge to my inner defenses. I would walk out of that office that day and I would drive us all home with nary a tremble of my lip, and I would repress the sorrow and the anger and the rage building inside me for fairly long stretches of time, but I could not indefinitely hold the feelings at bay.

One May evening Maureen was not at home. This, in itself, was unusual: her unbendable concentration on Aidan was seldom broken; she took very little time for herself. With her off to the store, I held Aidan on my lap, the two of us on the sofa facing the twilight through the big picture window. A lullaby wafted out of the tape player. He was content and settled—a sweet moment. Everything seemed possible. Suddenly his head and shoulders jerked forward. I knew what was coming. The jolting seizures came more frequently, enveloping this whole body, folding him in on himself. His legs shot up to his chest, his arms thrust out in front of him. Fifteen seconds rest, and then a violent repeat. He did not cry but looked about for the source of his torment. I sat and held him, utterly helpless. All I could do was speak to him, try to comfort him with the sound of my voice. The phenobarbital was not due for another four hours. There was nothing to do but wait it out. And as it subsided, the wash of my tears spilled down his tiny chest and the gasps of my despair rose up into the emptiness.

The image of a flood comes to mind. A tumultuous rising of a river above danger level. Water spilled over its banks, fields filled with muddy torrents, the geography of everyday life covered over by swirling streams. It caught us by surprise. We could see the current building but, before we knew it, we were pulled in, struggling to stay afloat, drifting at the mercy of the deluge. Resistance was futile; we could only move along with the surge and wait for the cataclysm to subside. But we would never find ourselves back on familiar ground. The river had been rerouted: the flood waters were so great that they did not return to their original channel but fell into a new course, leaving bare the old riverbed and drowning all that lay in their path.

When faced with such devastation, you call upon whatever personal resources you have, whatever will work to keep you afloat. For some, it may be the comfort of family, for others the transcendence of religion or the rationality of science.

Not for me. Beyond Maureen, I was not close to my family; God was not a significant part of my world view; and science seemed irrelevant to my personal and emotional tribulations. When in trouble, I looked elsewhere for answers and support. One alternative was the *Book of Changes*.

It is an ancient book, with links to mythical Chinese antiquity, taking its full form some time in the later Western Zhou Dynasty (1040–771 B.C.E.), perhaps in the ninth century before Christ. There is no single author; the text has been shaped by countless venerable thinkers, including Confucius. For centuries, the *Book of Changes* has functioned as an oracle, used by fortune tellers to divine the fate of curious questioners, kings and commoners alike. It is divided into sixty-four sections, each a multilayered concept—"The Creative," "The Receptive," "Holding Together," "The Taming Power of the Small." Each idea is represented by a hexagram, an arrangement of six broken or solid lines. The Creative's hexagram is made up of six solid lines, one above the other; The Receptive's is six broken lines; the sixty-two other hexagrams include every possible combination of six lines, broken and solid. A random selection of one these hexagrams, determined by drawing straws or flipping coins, provides a response to any question posed. The answers are indirect, invoking natural images ("clouds rise up to heaven: the image of Waiting") and cryptic ancient references ("it furthers one to cross the great water"). The best translations make the obscure text useful for personal, social, or even political purposes.

I had studied the *Book of Changes* in college, when my interest started to turn toward things Chinese. Politics and history had initially drawn me to China. I was captivated by the drama of the revolution and the tumultuous political transformations of the twentieth century: the collapse of the old imperial order, the rise of the Communist Party, the charismatic excesses of Mao Zedong. I had stumbled onto these compelling stories on my own when I read Edgar Snow's stirring *Red Star Over China* the summer before my junior year. The epic tales of war, rebellion, and survival carried me away—they would eventually become my life's work. Unfortunately, at the time my small college offered only one regular course on these subjects, which I took, longing for more. The only additional class on China was a chance offering one semester by a visiting professor of philosophy, a study of the naturalist teachings of Taoism. We began with the *Book of Changes*, which predates the Taoist classics but shares some of the same sensibilities.

The older oracle provides an opening onto the *Tao*, or Way, the centerpiece of Taoist thought and an integral part of other Chinese philosophies as well. The Way is, simply put, the complex unity of nature. It is not a transcendent God standing above and apart from His creation; it is more like a common, earthbound origin from which all things grow and are sustained. Each thing has its own character and particularity, yet all fit together into a variegated whole, an all-inclusive Way. One interpreter suggests it is like an uncultivated field. In winter its character is evident for all to see; it is simple and empty and still. In summer it is alive with a profusion of flowers and plants, covered over by the diversity it nurtures and unseen by admirers but silently holding on to its original qualities of simplicity, emptiness, and stillness. The underlying field expresses itself in the many plants that grow from it; and the plants, in all of their multiplicity, are extensions of the common ground beneath. While flowers grow and develop, the field itself appears to be doing nothing, but without it, nothing would be done. For Taoists, such subtleties in and of nature are models for human behavior and judgment.

The *Book of Changes*, when consulted, offers a glimpse of the Way at a particular time in a particular place. A hexagram is a figurative description of the present, a metaphorical view of the moment, generated at random but capturing the complex interplay of worldly context and personal need. It tells you where in the Way you are and what the best way forward might be.

In that one fortuitous college course, I learned how to select and read the hexagrams and I became something of a local fortune teller. Students in my hallway came to me with their problems—lovers, grades, careers—and I would use the enigmatic volume to divine their fates. Using the coin-toss method, I threw three pennies on the floor. Each heads was worth 3 and each tails, 2. The total for any given toss would be 6, 7, 8, or 9. The odd numbers signified a solid, *yang*, line; and the even numbers a broken, *yin*, line. If a throw yielded a 6 or a 9 (three 2's or three 3's), then that line was special: the *Book of Changes* included specific references for "pure *yang*" or "pure *yin*" lines. Six throws of the three coins produced six lines, a hexagram, corresponding to a concept and its ramifications, that could be found in the book. I then interpreted, as best I could, the remote text. For a woman uncertain how to tell her parents she was gay:

> *The superior man of devoted character*
> *Heaps up small things*
> *In order to achieve something high and great.*

In other words, bring them along slowly, don't make it a big confrontation. For a man with roommate trouble:

> *It furthers one to see the great man.*
> *Perseverance brings good fortune.*

We laughed that maybe this meant it was time for him to go to the Dean's Office! No one took this too seriously, myself included, but the ancient Chinese book did offer subtle insights into our predicaments; it gave us something to reflect upon as we struggled with our crises of young adulthood.

What impressed me most about the *Book of Changes* then, and has kept me returning to it over the years, was its reliance on chance. To access the text, one is supposed to engage in some sort of random choice. The reader does not analytically decide what to read, but is led to a particular passage by the luck of the draw. The form of choosing matters less than the experience of chance. In Chinese cities, there are fortune tellers huddled on side streets and back alleys who invent their own methods of random selection. In a Hong Kong night market, I once found a man with six small bamboo cages, each containing a small finch. For a price, I chose one of the birds. That cage was opened and the tiny creature hopped out and pulled a card from a deck arrayed before it. The card referred to a particular selection from the *Book of Changes* and my fortune was told. The birds were agents of chance and opened the way to the old book's advice.

Chance infuses the philosophy of the *Book of Changes*. It views life as fundamentally beyond our control, which has always seemed right to me. My life had taken some unexpected turns for the better in the years before Aidan's birth. I had worked hard, to be sure, but I was acutely aware that things could have turned out for the worse. Several graduate school friends were mired in dead-end jobs with little pay and no time to write; others had gone through painful divorces, their personal lives in shambles. Maureen and I were fortunate by comparison. And then, suddenly, we were on the other side of luck, struggling with our son's exceedingly rare birth defects. It felt like we were not independent movers, freely deciding our fate by ourselves; we were, rather, enmeshed in complex natural processes that irresistibly pushed and pulled at us. We were not masters of our circumstances, but servants of fortune. When I went to it, the *Book of Changes* reminded me of the contingency of our lives:

> *Human life on earth is conditioned and unfree, and when man recognizes this limitation, and makes himself depen-dent upon the harmonious and beneficent forces of the cosmos, he achieves success.*

There is optimism here. Fortune is not wholly capricious; there are patterns and cycles to nature—"forces of the cosmos"—and these suggest certain recurring themes and events in an individual existence. We are born, we grow, we thrive, we decline, we weaken, we die. However much we may want to deny our place in this grand procession, we cannot resist the inexorable changes of life. The trick is to know where you are at any given moment and what external forces are acting upon you.

I needed such counsel in the aftermath of Graham's pessimistic prognosis. "Nature is cruel," he had said, and we felt that something like cruelty was being perpetrated upon Aidan and us. It certainly seemed like something beyond our control was bringing on unwanted changes. I had thought I was going to be a father, just a regular sort of father, with all of the conventional fatherly requirements. I had prepared myself for that change, it seemed natural. Now my role had been quickly transformed into Father of Disabled Child, a different status, one that was harder to anticipate and freighted with dread and alienation. But maybe it was not just about the cruelty of nature; maybe there was comfort to be found not only in the essential cycles of light and dark, life and death, but also in our new and unsettling situation. This was the way the *Book of Changes* might help me.

Sitting silently at a battered desk I had brought from what seemed like another life, the time before Aidan's birth, I thought about what question to ask. Finding the right question was half the work. My inquiry had to capture the moment or the exercise would be futile; so I took my time and considered what I needed to know. I had learned over the years that the oracle was not well-suited to narrow or mechanistic questions. It offered the greatest insight into broader and more fundamental issues. But what was most important about Aidan's condition? My eyes wandered out the window of the second-floor study in our modest but comfortable house. A large box elder filled the view, its crown stretching up higher than its shallow roots seemed able to bear. It was a precarious tree, listing forward slightly, unsettled in the muddy ground. We had recently discovered that a major portion of its trunk was rotting away; it might not last much longer.

I asked: what will happen to him? What will become of Aidan? The question betrayed a certain mistrust of Graham's prognosis. Maybe the doctors were wrong; maybe Aidan would not be as severely compromised as they believed; maybe there was a greater chance of something approaching normality for Aidan. This was what I needed to know. If Graham were wrong, if Aidan could grow and develop, then I might dare to hope; I could ardently invest myself, without fear of emotional devastation, in the possibility of his improvement. But if Aidan was indeed fated to die soon, I would have to try to calibrate my feelings accordingly and prepare myself for the worst.

I threw the three pennies six times. The first line, starting from the bottom and working up, according to convention, was broken; the second solid. There followed broken, broken, solid, broken. No pure *yang* or *yin* lines. The coins pointed that day to "The Abysmal (Water)," the twenty-ninth hexagram. The image invoked was that of a ravine or a pit with water running through it. There was a clear sense of danger about it, fraught with the peril of rapids running through a narrow canyon. No exit was apparent and a false move could bring disaster—an apt description of our situation. I took it as an ominous portent. By emphasizing the danger of the situation, the *Book of Changes* appeared to be confirming Graham's prediction: we had been cast into an abyss with no easy escape. It looked like I would have to assume catastrophe was in the offing.

But the text was not entirely pessimistic; it did not dwell only on the danger, but pointed to a way out. Water was the key:

> *It flows on and on, and merely fills up all the places through which it flows; it does not shrink from any dangerous spot nor from any plunge and nothing can make it lose its own essential nature. It remains true to itself under all conditions.*

Water yields to its surroundings; it takes the shape and follows the course of the path it finds. Its adaptability gives it a certain resilience, its constancy a certain power—and it maintains these characteristics however precipitous its passage. Few of us can match these qualities, especially when facing something as trying as the discovery that a child will never run or sing or see. Our impulse is not to yield but to fight, to "rage, rage against the dying of the light." But most often we are bound by circumstance and there is freedom in moving, water-like, within and along the channel open to us, at least until the next danger.

I realized that the reading was not directly speaking to what would become of Aidan. It was answering another question, one that I had not asked but that was certainly turning in my mind, the question I had asked Graham: what should we do? The passage did not detail precisely how to adapt to danger, like the stream in the abyss, but it gave me a mental image of how to meet the challenge: take on the shape of the surroundings, fill up the places encountered, flow over and around the rocks and falls. I should not fight against Aidan's inevitable disability but embrace it, find what beauty there was and ride with that to a happier place. Worrying about whether or when he would die was beside the point; I had to accept the fact of his disability and adjust my plans and desires. There was hope in these words. If I could open myself to the situation, not force things, but just follow where Aidan was taking me, there was a way out of the abyss:

Water flows on uninterruptedly and reaches its goal...

By the summertime, after eight or nine months of anxiety, I felt like I was beginning to understand our situation, finding a way of managing the disappointments and fears. I could grasp in my intellect what was happening to Aidan and what might be required of us. I could read and understand both the scientific rationality of medical journals and the lyricism of the *Book of Changes*; I could learn pediatric neurology and Taoist thought. I can do this, I thought.

Then, one bright June day, I couldn't.

I was sitting on the living room floor, propped against the couch, listening to the afternoon radio news, eating grapes from a small bowl. Warm sunshine bathed the room, infusing everything with bright expectation. Comfortable in the familiar setting, I was happy: Aidan was nestled in naptime security, the day was beautiful, nothing threatened our familial peace. Everything was under control. Then, abruptly, Maureen walked in and asked, in a pointed voice, if I had given Aidan his seizure medicine, due an hour earlier. I had not and said so. She shot a hard glance at me and turned quickly into the kitchen to prepare the harsh red liquid. It was obvious she was mad that I had not done the job.

Just then something in me snapped. The sunshine was suddenly ineffectual, the atmosphere darkened. In a quick and violent motion I hurled across the room the small ceramic bowl I had been holding. It darted like a Frisbee, low and hard, into the dining room, and shattered loudly against the wall. The cat scrambled upstairs; the dog hopped to her feet. My face flushed and my hands trembled. A million terrible thoughts swirled in my head simultaneously, merging into a blurred mass of hostility. Not knowing where my anger might go next, Maureen walked down the hall to Aidan's room, leaving me alone in all of my rage. I did not carry on, however. That one forceful gesture seemed to be enough that time; it drained my animosity. My racing heart gradually settled back into its usual beat and I collected the shards of my ire.

I didn't know where the anger had come from. Though short and unfocused, it was out of proportion to the immediate events at hand. Maureen's question had set me off, it sparked something deep inside me, but I was not angry at her in any profound and lasting manner. She had pushed too hard at that moment, starkly laying bare my failure to attend to the medication, but I could not sustain anger toward her. Aidan's condition was testing us in ways we never expected, and we did not always know how to respond to one another, but we knew how to give each other individual sanctuary, when to disengage, when to drop the conversation and just get on with the pressing tasks at hand. The space we gave to each other, the silences we allowed, kept us intact. In the emptiness Maureen provided me by walking out of the room that day, I knew my anger was not about her.

Was it Aidan? Was I harboring resentment against him for turning my life upside down? I did not feel gloomy around him. When he was wrapped in my arms, his elbows drawn to his sides and his hands tucked to his chest, no burning irritation welled up from inside me. In fact, quite the opposite was true: his touch, his smile, his call, all of it enchanted me. Through all of the turmoil, he did not fuss too much, but usually sat serenely in his carriage or carrier, tranquil with himself and his surroundings. His peacefulness was infectious. Sitting with him settled on my lap put me at ease, diffused my anxieties. No, I could not be mad with him. He was, after all, perfectly innocent. It was not his fault that his brain was malformed; he had no part in his own undoing. Even if I grumbled late at night when he woke us for food or comfort, I could not, upon reflection, take him to task. He was a baby, beset by severe disability, doing his best to find his way.

That left me. I must have been angry with myself, but I did not know why. In the aftermath of my outburst, I was more confused and ashamed than knowing. What should I do? It was that same question again, the question I had posed to the doctor and to the oracle, but now it was more personal, focused more on me and my place in all that was unfolding around me. It seemed that, while I could learn much about science and philosophy, I did not yet know in my heart how to live this new life.

3.

The Knowing Are
Never Learned

Aidan was, in his own fashion, gaining some ground.

By nine months, his legs were becoming his best muscles and he was learning to use them to some effect. He could not crawl or sit or roll over, but he could kick. Sitting in a small blue vinyl chair, specially designed to provide support for his limp body, he would flash a devilish smile, brighten his eyes, and vigorously let fly with both legs, laughing all the while. In the bath, he would splash with great abandon, soaking whoever was there holding his head out of the shallow pool of soapy water. To encourage this activity, we hung wind chimes over his crib, low enough so that if he reared back and kicked up he would set them clanging and tingling. And he did. Wherever we were in the house, we could hear the happy sound of his purposive action.

He also seemed to be gaining a sense of his relationship to others. Using his voice, he drew us into a call-and-response game. "Ah...h...h..," he would announce, and we answered with the same. "Ah...Ah...Ah," he replied. We would go back and forth this way several times, he in his crib just across the hall from our room, all of us thrilled at mutual recognition. Maureen and I took this as the first stirrings of cognitive development. It was evident he knew our voices and understood that he could use his sounds to attract our attention and our response. I could see a spark of recognition in his face when Maureen spoke to him. Knowing his hearing was good, she would bathe him in her voice, talking to him constantly, singing, humming, cooing. He also gleamed when I made the special sound I used to announce my comings and goings, a high-pitched elephantine squeak. He could hear us, could sense the presence of his parents, and return the love we gave him.

None of this was in the handy baby development books, which, by that time, we had discarded. Aidan was taking his own time and growing in his own way, however idiosyncratic and uncharted. But whatever the progress, Graham's prognosis hovered ominously in the background.

While it was obvious that Aidan's developmental delay was significant—he still could not hold his head upright— we could not simply accept the terrible predictions. We needed another opinion. Maybe another doctor would see something different, have something more positive to say. We spoke with other parents of disabled children we had met in the past few months, people who, like us, were working their way through difficult medical mazes. The name of another pediatric neurologist came up several times, a man farther east toward Boston in a large university medical center, a man with experience in the most difficult cases, a fair and compassionate man, our new friends said. And so we went.

The appointment began routinely enough. We recounted Aidan's birth, the onset of the seizures, the developmental delay. Stressing the positive, we told the new doctor that Aidan was advancing on his own terms, that he worked valiantly to lift his head, to take control of his muscles. We tried to present Aidan as more than just an unusual neurological condition: he was a happy and loved little boy.

The new doctor listened to our story. He examined Aidan, testing reflexes, vision, muscle tone. Then, with hardly a break in his rhythm, he told us about a study, one showing that the best predictor of life span for severely disabled young adults was the ability to feed oneself. Use of a fork and spoon, the new doctor said with some fascination, was strongly correlated with longer life. This remark struck me as a non sequitur, with no discernable relation to Aidan, and the meeting deteriorated from there. This doctor did not have Graham's empathy and warmth. He spoke with a detached authority, a coldly precise expertise. It seemed as if he felt he had to be the bad cop to Graham's good cop, to be the one to drive home to us just how bad Aidan's condition was. And that is what he did. His words slapped at us like harsh and frigid torrents: Aidan would certainly die young; he would be severely mentally retarded, physically incapacitated, blind. Seizures, he said, could kill him at any moment. If a random electrical discharge affected the brain stem, all involuntary impulses would shut down, and breathing would stop. Death could come suddenly and surely. The new doctor noted how difficult such situations were for families and asked if we had thought about putting Aidan away in an institution.

We had no answer for him; there was nothing to say that could counteract the onslaught of bad news. He said much of what Graham had told us, with the unsettling addition of institutionalization, but he said it in a hard and uncaring voice. We thanked him and left quietly with a better understanding of the value of Graham's gentle manner.

Institutionalization was repellent to us. We did not talk much about it because we came to quick agreement against it. Aidan was still very young and his care was quite similar to that of a typical infant: changing his diaper, feeding him, bathing him. Of course, there were all of the medical complications. We had to administer and keep track of medications, take him to his many doctor's appointments, and find constructive therapies. But we could do all of this for ourselves from home. Maureen's nursing background and my relatively flexible work hours made it all fairly manageable, except for the fears and anxieties that would haunt us wherever Aidan resided.

The question of institutionalization was especially painful for Maureen. One of her cousins was severely disabled. He had been a healthy child with all of the usual faculties. One day, in the midst of playful rough-housing, he was hit on the head with a rock. The wound did not seem too serious at the time and did not require much by way of medical attention.

A few days later, however, he had a seizure and this began a relentless physical and mental decline. He lost motor skills and cognitive powers. It was the late 1950s and Maureen's aunt and uncle came under incredible pressure from medical professionals to "put him away." They resisted and cared for him at home, with virtually no help. There was no community outreach or home-based therapies, none of the supports, like Linda, that Maureen and I would find. They were alone but they did it because they believed in caring for their family themselves, regardless of the impact on their lifestyle.

When the cold, white-coated neurologist asked whether we had considered institutionalizing Aidan, Maureen instantly measured his overture against the experience of her aunt and uncle. They had sacrificed and struggled to keep their son at home, to avoid the horrendous conditions of the state hospitals. The 1970s scandal at Willowbrook, a New York City mental institution, confirmed their decision: secreted television images showed a bleak and forbidding place filled with neglected and abused patients, rocking aimlessly and alone in dirty rooms with caged windows. No, that would not be Aidan's fate.

I had not lived as closely to profound disability. My family had a smattering of mental illness, but none so serious as to require long-term institutionalization. Perhaps my great uncle Norman should have been placed in a hospital or home, but he never was. He was mentally retarded. My grandfather had tried to look after him but Norman would not accept much in the way of help. Any money he was given he either gave away or spent on drink for himself or gifts for others. He was famous for buying flowers and randomly handing them out to women as they passed by. The guys down at the auto body shop let him sleep in the back of their garage, and everyone in town came to know him as the Mayor, a benign street person who never harmed a soul. In fact, they erected a statue of him when he died: Norman Lane, Mayor of Silver Spring, Maryland.

Norman would occasionally embarrass the more conventional members of the family, but his adversity paled in comparison to Aidan's incapacity. My relatives and I had no point of reference for him; we were making every judgement and observation anew. Yet, even in this blank ignorance, it never seemed right to send Aidan away, to give him over to strangers. How could they ever love him more or care for him better than we would?

He would stay with us at home, his home, and we would listen for the wind chimes over his bed to jangle from his kicks and lift our spirits.

I was trained to explain. My research and writing and teaching had centered on discovering social scientific explanations for Chinese politics, and this carried over to my handling of Aidan's affliction. I could understand the doctors when they spoke in terms of correlations and probabilities and hypotheses. Much of the specific vocabulary was new to me—cerebral dysgenesis, congenital malformations, polymicrogyria—but the general grammar and syntax were familiar. The scientific method of searching for evidence to confirm or discount theoretical explanations was, in its most abstract form, what I did for a living. It was a style of thinking that I understood and practiced. On more than one occasion, a medical professional, after overhearing Maureen and I discussing some aspect of Aidan's care, would ask if I was a doctor. I could almost pass because my mind was used to scientific reasoning, and I was now well-versed in the details of Aidan's case.

Science could help him, I believed. Seizure medications, though they never completely stopped his multiform convulsions, probably limited the electrochemical disturbances in his brain. Maureen was distrustful of the drugs and sometimes wanted to cut back on them; but I always argued against any reduction, worried that biology might conspire against him and make things worse. I had witnessed psychosis, had taken the razor blade out of my friend's hand as she ranted about how Fiedel Castro was plotting to hurt her and how she had to go to Cuba now. Lithium finally chased these demons from her head; the chemistry worked, I knew that. Maybe the chemistry was also working for Aidan in ways we could not see. I believed that it could.

But my acceptance of science extended only so far. I would give him the anticonvulsant drugs and take him to the hospital, but I could not accede to the death sentence. When physicians intoned the grim dirge, predicting Aidan's early demise, I shut my ears and denied the validity of their explanations. I didn't care what the studies reported or what the probabilities were; none of it could tell me who this boy was, what he felt in his heart and what his life meant. Graham shied away from questions not strictly medical. The second neurologist had treated Aidan as a physical oddity and could only counsel us to shut him away. Neither of them offered any insights or suggestions into making the best of our predicament. Their science could not show us how to care for Aidan as a person, an individual more than the sum of his maladies. I was stunned by how quickly some could conclude that my son, not yet a year old, was hopeless, his life lost, and that he should be excluded from the love of his family and friends.

My rising discouragement with the mainstream medicine, an aproach that could only tell me what was wrong with Aidan but not what was right with him, rekindled in me the skepticism that had almost been extinguished by my graduate social science training. Why should I believe any of what the doctors said? None of us can fully know our future; chance moves in ways we cannot predict or wholly understand. I had been surprised by the unexpected turns in my own life; maybe Aidan's would change course and confound the pessimists. We had already strayed into the realm of infinitesimal probabilities, well beyond the pale of typical medical cases. There was no name for the odd combination of abnormalities that beset Aidan, no comparison groups in the vast computer data fields. We were in unknown territory; so how, then, could the doctors know where we were headed? How could anyone?

Having crashed into the limits of science, I was again drawn back to ancient Chinese philosophy in search of a different, perhaps more positive, perspective on Aidan. Dusting off my old college copy of the *Tao Te Ching*, the foundational (fourth century B.C.E.) text of Taoism attributed to a legendary man called Lao Tzu, I found a start.

Longing to take hold of all beneath heaven and
      improve it...
I've seen such dreams invariably fail.
All beneath heaven is a sacred vessel,
something beyond all improvement.
Try to improve it and you ruin it.
Try to hold it and you lose it.

For things sometimes lead and sometimes follow,
sometimes sigh and sometimes storm,
sometimes strengthen and sometimes weaken,
sometimes kill and sometimes die.

And so the sage steers clear of extremes,
clear of extravagance,
clear of exultation.
(29)

Isn't that what science tries to do: take hold of all beneath heaven and improve it? The chemists and biologists and physicists and the rest first strive to apprehend the world, to categorize it, analyze it, and theorize it, and then they try to act upon it, to change it, shape it, improve upon it. That is the grand scientific task. But Lao Tzu, who may or may not have actually existed, scoffs at this conceit. *All beneath heaven,* the riotous diversity of earthly nature—humanity included—defies improvement. It is not that the world is perfect as it is, just that it has certain ineffable ingredients that cannot be captured by simplistic devices of reason and logic. Some scholars translate the original Chinese text as "numinous vessel," instead of "sacred vessel," implying the formless and infinite qualities of nature. Any attempt to act upon all beneath heaven, to dominate it with science, will fail: *try to hold it and you lose it.* Millennia before Werner Heisenberg mathematically recognized that intervening in nature changes nature, the uncertain figure of Lao Tzu was celebrating a more radical uncertainty principle of his own.

From this vantage point, the judgments rendered by the physicians—the devaluation of Aidan's life—were mistaken. Of course, Aidan was unusual physically. There were many basic things he could not do: see, crawl, sit up, stand. Perhaps he might even die young. Yet these differences did not mean he was something alien and extraneous, they did not justify his exclusion from society. Quite to the contrary, if the totality of all under heaven was a sacred or numinous vessel, then he was an element of that unimprovable unity. He was part of it. Indeed, the indispensability of the abnormal and the weak and the disabled is a central tenet of Taoism.

All beneath heaven knows beauty is beauty
only because there's ugliness,
and knows good is good
only because there's evil.

Being and nonbeing give rise to one another,
difficult and easy complete one another,
long and short measure one another,
high and low fill one another,
music and noise harmonize one another,
before and after follow one another:

that's why a sage abides in the realm of nothing's own
    doing,
living out that wordless teaching.
The ten thousand things arise without beginning there,
abide without waiting there,
come to perfection without dwelling there.

Without dwelling there: that's the one way
you'll never lose it.
(2)

Two things jump out of this passage. First, it would be perfectly in keeping with the spirit of the text to say that ability and disability belong to one another; each constitutes the other. Disabled people are not marginal to the human experience; they are central to it, for without them there could be no definition of ability. The eugenicists are quite literally inhuman, and unnatural, to believe that physical irregularities should be eradicated. To do so would rob humanity of essential constituents.

The second point of this quotation is a suggestion of how to understand the importance of maintaining the tension of opposites in nature. Lao Tzu says that the person who wants to understand all under heaven, the unity of which is the Way, abides in the realm of nothing's own doing. In other words, the wise man does nothing. He allows things to follow their own course, without interfering in the movements of nature. He does not work against the Way. This is not a conscious effort, a calculated inaction, for that would be to "dwell" and not simply "abide." Knowledge of the Way, and the place of Aidan in it, would come not from intentional scientific study of the facts of his case; it would be gained by open-minded perception of his presence. You cannot strive to learn it; you have to come to know it. Without dwelling there: that's the one way you'll never lose it.

But I was trained to explain. Everything I was reading in the *Tao Te Ching* was pushing against my impulse to talk the science talk. I could see the beauty of the passages but I could not give my mind and heart over to the ideas. What would I say when a neurologist was suggesting a new drug regimen to control seizures? Should I serenely remark, "Oh, let's just abide in the realm of nothing's own doing...?" And even if I could find the conviction to utter such a thing, would that be tantamount to giving up on Aidan? Would doing nothing worsen his condition and hasten his death?

However natural that might be, I could not abide the thought.

Maureen, too, was becoming disillusioned with the doctors. From her work as a nurse in various settings—large medical centers, small-town hospitals, clinics, visiting nursing—she had developed a certain skepticism about the ways of conventional American medicine. She had seen too many instances where a hyper-scientific ethos undermined good patient care. Too often, doctors focused on specific conditions, not whole persons. Powerful drugs and aggressively invasive surgeries, while necessary at times, were too quickly invoked. She knew we would have to do such things for Aidan,but she had a nagging feeling that more and better could be done.

Linda told her about a young couple who did massage therapy based upon principles of Chinese acupuncture. By touching and gently manipulating certain points on the body, the masseur or masseuse could relax or invigorate an ailing person in a variety of ways, or so it was claimed. It seemed a reasonable thing for Aidan. Perhaps acupressure would do some good for his listless limbs and developmental delay. At best they might spark some positive physical progress; at worst, they would give him a soothing massage. So, one fall day, we went to see them.

Stan and Mary, the massage therapists, lived and worked over the mountains to the East, about an hour's drive. It was a pleasant trip, through thick forests, along a leaping highland stream, past picturesque farms and charming small towns. Their office took up the first floor of a good-sized Victorian house. We entered through the old country kitchen. The central dining room had been transformed into a small waiting area and registration desk, painted in warm off-whites. In the rooms beside and behind it were padded therapy tables, short stools on rollers, and small bookcases with various publications on massage therapy and its more esoteric relatives: rolfing, shiatsu, reiki, and the like. In one of the rooms was a chart of a human body marked with acupuncture points and "energy meridians," a central concept of traditional Chinese medicine. Soft New Age music suffused the air. There were no macramé wall hangings, but there could have been.

It was a relaxing place but I was ill at ease, unwilling to uncritically embrace the scene. Maureen was more focused. The connotations of the place did not matter to her: if this was going to help Aidan then she was going to do it.

The receptionist showed us into the therapy room directly behind her desk. It had once been the front parlor of the old house, trimmed with stylized oak molding around the windows and doors. Without being told, we stretched Aidan out on the therapy table.

He was just to his first birthday and had been growing steadily. His size created an impression of a strong and solid body, precisely the opposite of the reality he lived.

Stan came in after a few minutes. His beard was a little longer and more unkempt than mine; his bushy hair clipped the top of his collar. I guessed, to myself, that he was a few years younger than us. He looked intently into our eyes as he introduced himself; the steadiness of his gaze suggested conviction and determination. His hands were large and strong. We told him our story: the agony of Aidan's tenth day of life; the revelation of his multifaceted disabilities; our growing frustration with powerful drugs and unhelpful physicians. It was a tale we had told many times.

Listening closely and nodding occasionally, Stan jotted down some notes. He seemed immediately to understand our situation. Indeed, he told us that he and his wife had faced similar circumstances. Their daughter, Carrie, had been born with low muscle tone and developmental delay. Doctors had given them dire predictions of serious disability. She would most likely never walk, the experts said. Stan and Mary had worked with Dr. Graham, and found him aloof and unwilling to look beyond the medical conditions; he did not see Carrie in the fullness of herself. Deeply discouraged but determined to help their daughter, they left Graham, minimizing their engagement with conventional medicine, and turned instead to a combination of alternative approaches. Stan told us of how they worked for hours, day in and day out, pressing and stretching Carrie's little body. He showed us a picture of an obviously energetic five-year-old in joyful movement. Not only could Carrie walk, she could dance and sing and read her alphabet. She was a typical little girl.

Stan called Mary in to meet us. She was early thirty something, the still-youthful glow of her face hardly dulled by small wrinkles around her eyes. There was a seriousness of purpose about her, but she was not stern. Quite the contrary, she radiated empathy and compassion. She smiled at Aidan, who was still stretched out on the therapy table, and stroked his arm. Confirming Stan's story about their daughter, Mary assured us that there were ways of reaching Aidan, of bringing him out of his limitations. They could help us.

It was uncanny. Here was a couple who appeared to have lived our life. They had struggled through the terrible news of a disabled child and had overcome a gloomy prognosis. Maybe with their support, we, too, could make a better life for Aidan.

Stan then turned to the work before him. He sat on a wheeled stool next to the table and placed his large hands on Aidan's small body. As he moved his fingers over Aidan's chest and sides, he spoke of energy fields and pathways. It was not just about loosening up muscles or improving blood flow. It was about channeling qi—the Chinese term for the body's essential energy—and repatterning the natural forces that coursed through Aidan's tissues. Stan did not vigorously knead Aidan's skin but touched him very lightly, explaining that by placing two fingers on this particular point and two more at another spot he was causing a certain flow of energy. The talk lapsed into neurology when Stan suggested that new nerve connections could actually be generated through the right combination of touch and repeated movement. If we wanted Aidan to improve the use of his arms and hands, we needed to first open certain energy meridians and then induce movement of those body parts. This would literally rewire the brain and nervous system, bringing the parts in question to useful life. Carrie was the living testament to the efficacy of the therapy.

Maureen and I listened and watched. We asked what we could do at home to build upon whatever effect Stan's work might be having. When we left, after a hour of talk and touch, we had a sense of possibility unlike anything the medical doctors had ever given us.

At home, we followed their advice. With Aidan on a blanket on the floor, we gently touched and caressed his back and arms and legs. The exercises were similar to the standard range-of-motion stretching that Linda and the other physical therapists practiced on Aidan. But there were differences. The touch was lighter. The approach was sometimes opposite our usual ways: if we wanted to encourage Aidan to sit up, we did not push him up from behind; rather, we softly placed a hand on his stomach to draw his energy and attention forward and inward. To make him turn to his right, we did not push him from the left, but drew him toward the right with our touch. The aim was to animate his muscles, power up his nerves, transform his weakened body and start him toward conscious and meaningful movement.

We mentioned our foray into massage therapy to Graham the next time we saw him. A tight, thin smile etched across his face when we mentioned Stan and Mary. He did not say anything bad about them, but neither did he endorse their work. Instead, he spoke of "patterning," a therapy taken up in the 1950s and 60s. The idea was to continually move impaired limbs, back and forth, up and down, for hours a day, every day, in hope of stimulating the brain to reconnect with the forgotten muscles and make them useful. It was a strict regimen and, Graham said, it did not work. He told us that a few people who went through the treatment gained some new mobility, but it was not clear that this was due to patterning or whether it was simply unique and non-replicable circumstances of individual cases. He was quite confident that neural pathways could not be created by physical manipulation.

While he was obviously skeptical of what Stan and Mary might be able to do for Aidan, Graham was restrained in his criticism. He did not pronounce solemnly that they were quacks or that acupressure would divert our attention from more effective treatments. Perhaps he knew that his own brand of medicine offered us little hope, which we needed desperately. Being a gentle man, he did not want to rob us of a constructive outlet for our anxiety. The massage therapy gave us something positive to do, something beyond helpless observation, and, as long as it was generally harmless, Graham was not going to ward us off absolutely.

We took Aidan to Stan and Mary every couple of weeks. They moved their office out of the Victorian house and into a renovated factory building. The large spaces, rough brick walls and high ceilings lent a new sense of openness and possibility to the sessions. But Aidan was not responding much at all. He would sometimes move in sync with the massage, stretching onto his back from his side or curling in toward his stomach, but his freshly aroused energy meridians were not producing significant changes in his muscle tone or his overall control of his body. His arms and trunk sagged when we held him. Well beyond his first birthday, he still could not lift his head. If there were any gains at all, they were meager.

As the months rolled by, Maureen and I became more and more discouraged. We never quite said it to each other directly, but both of us were beginning to feel guilty that Aidan's lack of progress was somehow our fault. Stan and Mary's enthusiasm and optimism were having a perverse effect on us. The more they spoke of improvement and how their little Carrie had fought through her affliction, the more we felt we were failing our boy. His lack of growth suggested that we were not doing the therapy properly; or we were not doing it often enough; or something. Or—and this was even harder to face—the severity of Aidan's condition was such that he would never, regardless of what we did, develop any further. Whatever the case, the expectation of advancement engendered by Stan and Mary was pressing down on us. The further the reward receded, the heavier a burden it became. We soon stopped going to see them.

I was driven by my desire to do something to make Aidan better but the *Tao Te Ching* challenged my fatherly instincts:

Way is perennially doing nothing
so there's nothing it doesn't do.

When lords and emperors abide by this
the ten thousand things follow change of themselves.

Desire drives change
but I've stilled it with uncarved nameless simplicity.

Uncarved nameless simplicity
is the perfect absence of desire,
and the absence of desire means repose:
all beneath heaven at rest of itself.
(37)

A friend had another idea. She knew of a man, Gabriel, who practiced something called craniosacral therapy, a gentle massage technique which sounded to me, at first, rather like the acupressure we were gradually giving up. Craniosacral care was different and would be beneficial, she assured us, and Gabriel was a trustworthy man. Again, we set off in search of something better for Aidan.

Gabriel lived further to the East than Stan and Mary. His home and office were on the other side of the Connecticut River, about a third of the way to Boston from our small purple valley in the northwest corner of Massachusetts. It was early spring when we first made the trip there; Aidan was about a year and a half old. The woods that surrounded Gabriel's house were scattered with snow and the unpaved driveway slick with mud. We sloshed into to a small waiting room at the back of the new, modern home and sat.

It did not take long before a tall, lean man, with a beard thinner than mine and a receding hairline, came down from the living quarters above and introduced himself to us. Gabriel moved easily and gracefully, the result, we would later learn, of years of studying the martial art of Aikido. His voice was soft, his manner gentle. He ushered us into another room, a bright, sunny space, newly constructed. Crystals hung in the windows. A padded therapy table took up most of the center of the room, alongside of which was a small stool on wheels. Odd knickknacks cluttered a small bookcase, which held an assortment of volumes not unlike those at Stan and Mary's place. I felt a certain misgiving creep up my back.

Gabriel asked us to stretch Aidan out on the therapy table. He inquired into Aidan's condition and we recounted for him the story of our continuing journey through conventional medicine. Rolling on the wheeled stool around to Aidan's head, he began to tell us something about craniosacral massage. It had something to do with the spinal fluid, which flows from the base of the backbone, or sacrum, to the head, or cranium; hence: craniosacral. Apparently, this fluid has a distinct pulse, unrelated to either blood pressure or respiration. By very gently touching the backbone, especially the neck, and the skull, the craniosacral pulse can be detected and ever so slightly manipulated. Maintaining the proper flow of spinal fluid could, Gabriel suggested, have wide-ranging health benefits.

I did not know what to make of what he was saying. It seemed plausible, and not quite so unusual as Chinese energy meridians, but if its effectiveness could be objectively demonstrated, then why was it relegated to only a small network of practitioners? Why was it not integrated into mainstream neurology?

As the questions bounced in my head, Gabriel snapped on some relaxing music, again reminiscent of Stan and Mary's, and slid his hands under the base of Aidan's skull, where the head meets neck. He made a cradle with his hands, fanning his fingers out along the upper most reaches of Aidan's spine. The child rested comfortably in his palms. Holding this position, Gabriel reported aloud his assessment of Aidan's craniosacral pulse. It was blocked and irregular, he said, and would require some work to make it right. He also noticed that Aidan's face was asymmetrical: one cheek bone was slightly higher than another, twisting his face up ever so slightly. This was important because the alignment of the skull bones could have an effect on the overall health of the craniosacral system.

I did not really understand any of this but was noticing that all Gabriel was really doing was holding the back of Aidan's neck and applying an imperceptible amount of pressure against his spinal column. It was very subtle. But was it really doing anything?

After an hour, the session ended with Gabriel suggesting we return in a week or two. He said that Aidan might be more alert and attentive as a result of that day's work. No other predictions or promises were stated or implied. He did not say that this therapy would transform Aidan fundamentally. Nothing was said about Aidan standing or walking or overcoming his mental retardation. We would just see how he responded.

As spring bloomed into summer, we fell into a fairly regular schedule of visits to Gabriel. Some effects of the craniosacral massage were becoming obvious. The treatment clearly soothed Aidan, bringing out of him deep sighs of release and repose. On more than one occasion, we took Aidan into the therapy room crying from some discomfort that he could not articulate and, after a very short time resting in Gabriel's hands, he would slip into a near-sleep, a serene stillness. This was more than we had seen with the acupressure, and was quite obviously a good thing for him. In addition, Aidan's face was noticeably more balanced, the alignment of his cheeks uniform and well-proportioned. Gabriel had eased the cranial bones into shape with the gentle but persistent press of his hands.

One day, while we sat alongside the table as Gabriel held Aidan's head, we noticed that Aidan was straining to turn to the right. He twisted his neck and pushed with all of his might to get himself moving in that direction, but his disobedient body did not follow. Gabriel remarked that it appeared that Aidan was attempting a rebirth, a repeat of his entrance into the world, and he asked if we wanted to work through it with him. Maureen and I looked at each other. She nodded in agreement and I stifled my doubt.

Gabriel instructed us to slide our hands under Aidan's back as he lay on the table, Maureen on one side and me on the other. Gabriel stayed at his head. Then, we were to simply follow Aidan's inclinations. If he moved to the right, we were to push him gently that way. Whatever he did, we did.

Aidan continued to press his head down and to the right and we eased his body over, slowly twirling him between us in the air. Off the end of the table we went, letting him move through space, down and around and over, supported all the while by our hands. All of this happened in slow motion, the three of us straining to position ourselves and facilitate Aidan's bodily freedom. After a good fifteen minutes, we had worked ourselves back to the table and Aidan gave out a great sigh and let loose the burden of his unruly muscles. He drifted into sleep.

Gabriel explained that disruptions in the craniosacral pulse are sometimes caused by the trauma of birth. Twisting and turning down the birth canal can compress the spine and skull, jamming and jarring delicate membranes and connections. A rebirth experience, like the one Aidan just enacted, could help recalibrate the system. It was also a spiritual reconnection, starting over with a new orientation of body and mind.

I watched as Aidan rested on the therapy table and found myself silently resisting Gabriel's explanation; my suspicion was too deep, my desire for more conventional answers too ingrained. I could not easily accept that I had just witnessed a physical/spiritual rebirth. On the other hand, there was Aidan, more comfortable than when we came. This was a victory in itself. I decided to strike a compromise with myself: I admitted that Gabriel was doing something good for Aidan, but I rejected the New Age interpretation. It was good but for some other, unknown reasons.

Dr. Graham had suggested we consult genetic counselors to help us determine whether heredity played some part in Aidan's disability and whether we should try to have more children. Hoping that science might still offer us some better news, we drove to Springfield to see them.

The chief geneticist, a woman of about fifty, was friendly and open; her assistant, a younger woman, careful and efficient. They took a blood sample from Aidan to do some preliminary screening and they asked us about our family histories. Were any relatives afflicted like Aidan? Had any died young? What were the causes of death of others? They measured Aidan's facial features and took note of all of his physical attributes: the light brown birth mark on his right thigh, the size of his hands, the swirl in his hair. Probing and noting, they went on for some time, but more gently than the second neurologist. They were warm toward Aidan, speaking to him, remarking upon his charm, elevating him to personhood.

In the end, however, they could not give us definite answers. They were able to rule out one genetic condition, Fragile-X Syndrome, but beyond that they could not say. It was not clear whether Aidan's condition was imprinted in our genes. Their best guess was that there could be as much as a one-in-four chance that any other child of ours would be severely disabled. One in four. That did not mean that Aidan was the one and the next three were likely to be risk free. It meant that every pregnancy could hold a 25 percent probability of disaster. If we were to try again, the happy expectant months would be replaced by week upon week of unremitting worry. It was impossible to contemplate at a time when every medical report was depressingly negative.

They scared me off the idea of another child. The anger was still inside me, it still burst forth unexpectedly, sometimes for no apparent reason. A stressful pregnancy might send me over the edge. Maureen was, at times, despondent from continual recomfirmations of Aidan's poor prognosis. What would another physically and mentally impaired child do to her? My sense was that neither of us, nor both of us together, could handle it. Maureen, however, was willing to run the risk. If there was no clear genetic cause of Aidan's problems, then who was to say another child might be just fine? But "one in four" kept echoing in my mind, so we avoided the topic and focused on Aidan's care.

The geneticists' way of thinking, however, bugged me. They were obviously conscientious professionals and good doctors, but it was precisely their confined expertise that bothered me. All they could understand of Aidan was derived from a series of questions and procedures defined by the standards of their field. Although they could learn something about him in this manner, they could not know very much, at best only a qualified probabilistic statement: we cannot rule out a 25 percent chance... This was yet another reminder of the deficiency of science. All their discipline would allow was the reduction of Aidan, or his future siblings, to a risk factor. Perhaps there was some truth in it, but it represented only a fraction of who he was. It said nothing of his smile or his happiness; it made no reference to the love he brought to us and out of us; it was a sadly incomplete picture of him or any other child, of whatever abilities, we might have. A line from the final section of the *Tao Te Ching* sprang to my mind:

The knowing are never learned
and the learned never knowing.

4.

Moving as One and the Same

As Aidan grew bigger, it was harder to watch other parents with typical children. Happily chattering words and phrases, stumbling around on drunkard's legs, the toddlers in our town all seemed to be advancing inexorably through the stages of childhood development. Their bodies were agile, their minds alert. They spilled their milk, made wild-eyed demands and generally drove their parents to distraction. We longed for such chaos, but it never came. Aidan's unchanging condition was still dominated by what he could not do and, with each passing month, the contrast with his peers grew more obvious and oppressive.

We decided to try to have another child. This was not a rash decision. It was not taken simply in response to the comparisons we made with other families. The odds that something would go seriously wrong a second time were one in four; one quarter of our luck was bad from the start. The figures were too worrisome to allow vanity to intrude on our thinking: we could not be anxious about our loss of the ideal family. Yet even with these frightful numbers, we had to try.

Watching other children made us realize that having an active, energetic boy or girl might remake our family dynamic; it might counterbalance the stresses and strains of Aidan's medical problems. We all needed more laughter and exuberance. A typical child could bolster our spirits and increase the circle of love surrounding Aidan. We had to try.

The uncertainties of another pregnancy had already led us to consider adoption. We looked into the possibilities of a Chinese baby. When we had lived there, we had met people connected to orphanages; it would have been easy to come home with a little girl (they do not give up their boys). But we were not ready then. We had been trying to plan carefully for the entry of a child into our lives and our circumstances were not quite settled enough at that time. Now, the year after Aidan's birth, everything was different. Adoption seemed safer, a haven from the perils predicted by the geneticists. So we went off to meet with a woman in the southern part of our rural county, out a country road in a big old farmhouse. She was a counselor, linked by phone and computer to various agencies and organizations for international adoptions. We filled out her forms and talked with her about who we were and why we wanted to adopt. Aidan was with us, asleep in his stroller, silently defining our purpose.

The walls of the office were adorned with pictures of happy multiracial families: Africans, Asians, Latin Americans, Russians, Romanians, all sorts mixed together in a colorful array of smiling nuclear-family salad bowls. Outside, the day was sunny and warm, early fall had not yet turned the deep greens into browns and yellows and dark reds. It was all pleasant enough. But it was evident that a foreign adoption would be a long and troublesome process. We had watched other couples go through it: being told one day that a child had been found for them, only to hear shortly afterward that the arrangements had fallen through. It would be even more arduous if we wanted a Chinese child. The government there had just announced a halt in all foreign adoptions to review and centralize their national policies. We left the counselor's place with more trepidation than when we had arrived.

I don't know what it was that finally steeled us to try another pregnancy. Our families were not pressuring us in any way. There was little in the way of social expectation. The one exception was a retired pediatrician who regularly sat in on my classes. When I had told him the full extent of Aidan's disabilities he commiserated for a moment and then abruptly retorted:

"Have another one; it would be the best thing for all of you."

A long moment passed between us as I absorbed his pronouncement. Maybe he was right. Maybe it was so obvious that everyone could see it, but only he had the courage to say it. My fears were still strong enough, however, to keep me from agreeing with him that day. He apologized later for being so forward. No one else ever said anything about more children. Our decision was not induced by others. It came from within each of us. There was no specific event or rationale that finally moved us. It was the slow and steady triumph of hope over risk. The probabilities were worrisome, but the gain could be immeasurable. We took the odds.

The pregnancy had to be watched closely. At sixteen weeks, we went for a special, high-powered sonogram that could detect if some of the brain malformations that had happened to Aidan were happening again. The specialists were in Lexington, all the way across the state. We set off with a certain foreboding, not saying too much to each other. Without discussing it at length, Maureen had made it clear to me that if there were problems, she was ready to go forward and have the child. I was less certain. It was impossible for me to see how we could manage a second severely disabled child; we were already seriously frayed. But neither could I find it in myself to press for an abortion against Maureen's conviction. It was not a carefree drive to Lexington.

Happily, the special sonogram was fine; there were no indications of anything out of the ordinary. Thereafter, the pregnancy unfolded uneventfully, with Maureen ballooning out to marvelously absurd proportions. With about two weeks to go, we were both feeling safe enough to take a rare night out. The respiratory therapist who had helped save Aidan during that first terrible episode came to baby-sit. She was one of the few people Maureen would allow to watch Aidan in her absence. With her at his bedside, we went to a wedding reception. In the giddiness of the evening we danced some vigorous polkas and Maureen's water broke the next day, a much more agreeable way to induce labor than the usual drugs. The day after that, Maureen's obstetrician ordered her in for a cesarean delivery.

We had asked the sonogram technicians not to reveal to us the baby's sex. So it came as a pleasant surprise as I watched the doctors deliver a girl, Margaret, on a snowy February day. She was pink and firm and vigorous. I could tell almost immediately that she would not have her brother's difficulties. On the very first day of her life, she strained to hold up her head and succeeded beyond what Aidan had been able to accomplish in his two years and four months. Hope, it seemed, had indeed prevailed.

Margaret was strong; Aidan was weak. We had no good explanation for the difference; no one could tell us why things had turned out this way. The geneticists remained noncommittal. Their general probabilities, if true, could not account for any particular child; Margaret's health did not change our chances for another disabled child, just as Aidan's affliction had had no bearing on Margaret. Dr. Graham did not think it was genetic anyway, believing instead that whatever had happened to Aidan was wholly random, not to be repeated, a lightning bolt out of the blue. While this might have been a sufficient conclusion for his medical analysis, for us it was just a beginning. We had to live daily with the growing contrast between our children, watching as Margaret moved up and through the many developmental milestones Aidan never reached, and wondering why, coming from the very same origins, they were so utterly different.

As the apparently inexplicable disparities mounted, I started to read Chuang Tzu, one of the most famous ancient Taoist writers. He is different from Lao Tzu, the mythical author of the *Tao Te Ching*. First of all, there probably was a man named Chuang Tzu (circa third century B.C.E.) and he probably was the witty and astute writer of the book that bears his name. His style and interpretation of Taoism is distinct as well. Lao Tzu lays out the key elements of Taoist thought but, for him, they are aimed not just at the individual seeking an understanding of life, but also at the statesman concerned with ruling a country. The *Tao Te Ching* is very much a primer on good government ("ruling a country is like cooking a small fish;" i.e., handle with care); it has an explicitly political side to it. Chuang Tzu, by contrast, mostly avoids politics and statesmanship. His writings are more focused on personal struggle and enlightenment, with a good deal of humor and absurdity along the way. He takes the poetic insights of the *Tao Te Ching* and runs with them, scripting vignettes and aphorisms that turn the meaning of Taoism inward, toward the deepest human needs. My circumstances seemed custom-made for a close reading of Chuang Tzu.

This was something new for me. I had never read Chuang Tzu in college or after. We did not get to it in that one class I took, so long ago. So, when I turned to it after Margaret was born, the text was fresh and absorbing. What

I noticed right away was the inclusiveness of Chuang Tzu's worldview:

> ...the real is originally there in things, and the sufficient is originally there in things. There's nothing that is not real and nothing that is not sufficient.
>
> Hence, the blade of grass and the pillar, the leper and the ravishing beauty, the noble, the sniveling, the disingenuous, the strange—in Way they all move as one and the same. In difference is the whole; in wholeness is the broken. Once they are neither whole nor broken, all things move freely as one and the same again.

Everything is real and sufficient unto itself. A seemingly broken child who cannot walk or talk or see is, in his own way, whole. He is a distinct entity but, at the same time, he fits into the kaleidoscopic totality of the world at large. In the grand sweep of the Way, Aidan has his place and, in this regard, is really no different than Margaret. On any tree there are straight and beautiful branches as well as those that are bent and gnarled, and, when looking at the tree as a whole, they move as one and the same. Chuang Tzu was telling me how to find peace with my two ostensibly different children.

> Only one who has seen through things understands moving freely as one and the same. In this way, rather than relying on your own distinctions, you dwell in the ordinary.

I, and everyone around me, was drawing distinctions between Aidan and Margaret, based upon their obvious physical and mental differences and our immediate understanding of how Aidan's disabilities would keep him from living up to our expectations of a normal life. But Chuang Tzu was urging us to see through conventional notions, let go of our hopes and fears, and *dwell in the ordinary*. The plain and direct fact of Aidan's presence alone, he seemed to be saying, would yield its own good. We just had to have the patience and compassion to see ourselves through to it.

A week after Margaret was born, Aidan came down with pneumonia. It was not the first time it happened to him, but it was worse than the time before. The doctors had long warned us that he would be prone to pneumonia; his low muscle tone made it hard for him to keep secretions from slipping into his lungs and blooming into serious infections. Fortunately, it had not occurred as often as predicted because he did not contract many colds and was generally resistant to bugs. On this day, however, it was clear that he was in dire straits.

When he awoke that morning, he never really perked up but remained listless for an hour or so. It was then we noticed that he was feverish and breathing laboriously. The skin in the crook of his neck, just under the Adam's apple, retracted as he inhaled, a classic sign of respiratory distress. His nostrils flared and he strained to pull air into his congested chest. Maureen listened to him with her stethoscope but had trouble distinguishing whether the problem was in his upper airway or down in his lungs; she was not used to diagnosing young children. Her mind was already made up, however. We were off to the doctor directly.

Luckily, Maureen's parents were visiting and could watch Margaret while we attended to Aidan. He was admitted to our small local hospital right away and put on intravenous fluids and antibiotics. Copious dosages of ibuprofen and acetaminophen were prescribed in an effort to bring down the fever, which posed a grave risk of seizures. We had been having fairly good luck controlling his convulsions with a new drug that had come on the market about six months earlier, but a persistent fever could destroy all of that, casting us back into neurological crisis. The hometown pediatricians knew this, of course, and they were quick to take preventive measures. They were worried, though, because Aidan was an intricate and intense case.

When it was evident that the essentials of Aidan's care were arranged, I returned home to manage the daily dance of tending to Margaret, going to work, and spelling Maureen at the hospital. One of us was always with Aidan. We could not leave him alone, anywhere. Maureen knew all too well what could go wrong in a hospital, and she absolutely demanded that one of us be present at all times to make sure the nurses and doctors got it right. Unyielding was her determination to get Aidan through this illness without major complication. She only grudgingly let me substitute for her, worrying that

I did not have sufficient background to know what should be done but recognizing that she needed rest to heal her abdominal incision from Margaret's delivery. Margaret needed her, too; so, Maureen would go home for a few hours a day to nurse her and I stayed the second and third night, sleeping fitfully in a rocking chair by Aidan's side.

He had a rough time of it. An oxygen saturation monitor, a glowing light attached to his big toe, showed that he was not getting enough air through his lungs. The nurses set up an oxygen tent to envelop him in the vital gas. Made of flimsy clear-plastic cloth, the tent fit over his bed, leaving enough head room to prop him up in his special blue chair, which we brought from home. We discovered that his head position was critical. If we supported his flaccid neck, shifting his head slightly forward and to the right, the numbers on the oxygen monitor increased toward normal range; when his head fell back, the numbers decreased again. Seeing this, Maureen squeezed under the tent and wedged herself behind Aidan on the bed, holding his head at just the right angle to ease his breathing.

After three days, he started to look better. His lungs were clearing and he was able to breathe room air comfortably. The oxygen tent came down. I was sitting in the sun-drenched single room with him; Maureen was home with Margaret and her parents. My mind was focused on what we needed to do when we got him home, which, I assumed, would be the next day or, at most, the day after. We would have to continue the antibiotics and increase his fluids. I would have to squeeze some time here and there from my job to check in at home regularly and make sure Maureen was coping with Aidan's recovery, Margaret's demands, and her own healing.

It was then, out of the corner of my eye, I noticed Aidan twitch. It was an unusual movement, a quick jolt of the arms and head, yet unlike the myoclonic seizures I could easily recognize. I watched him closely but it wasn't until I thought it would not repeat, several minutes later, that it happened again. It was some kind of seizure. Maureen walked in at just that moment, happy from her time with her baby daughter. I did not have to say much; she could read the worry on my face. Aidan seized again. Maureen hit the call button and a nurse came in, only to rush back out to summon a doctor.

Two doctors arrived in short order. Although the seizures seemed to have stopped, we huddled together and came up with a plan of attack should they recur. This comforted me. I liked having a plan, a procedure to follow to give me a sense, however fleeting, that we were doing something to stop the rogue sparks in Aidan's brain. Maureen was not relieved. Her senses were super-charged: eyes wide, ears alert, she could have smelled or tasted a seizure even before it burst upon us. And so we waited, waited and watched, waited to see if it came again. We could not think of home now, only the unhappy possibility of medical emergency.

David, a respiratory therapist, came in and made sure all of his equipment was ready in case he was needed. A calm and clear-eyed man, he assessed Aidan to gain a baseline of information against which he could compare any changes.

We chatted. Maureen knew him. She knew just about everyone, having worked right upstairs for two years, and she held him in high regard. There was no tension in the room; David had a way of diffusing our anxiety with his easy manner and technical proficiency.

As we talked, David on one side of the head of the bed and I on the other, Aidan started having seizures again. They started out subtly. His eyes looked to the right and trembled in that position, a condition call "nystagmus." He stuck the end of his tongue out of his partially opened mouth and stiffened his arms and legs. For someone who did not know him, it might be difficult to see that this was a seizure, but Maureen and I were quick to realize what was happening. David stayed close, monitoring his breathing. We called for the nurse.

She was an older woman, nervous and lacking in self-confidence. The doctors were gone and had left orders for what to do if the seizures started again, but she was the person responsible for assessing the situation and taking action. We urged her to give him the phenobarbital that was the first line of defense, and after hesitating for a minute or two, she did. Maureen was deeply anxious. She knew this nurse, knew that she was weak on technique and slow to decision.

The medication did not immediately affect Aidan. He continued to stare shakily to his right, away from me and toward David. His lips remained pursed, his limbs tense. David kept close track of his breathing, which was shallow and uneven. After fifteen long minutes of this, we began to let down our guard. Things were not markedly improving but neither were they getting noticeably worse. The pheno-barbital would soon be fully effective and might be sufficient to calm Aidan's nervous system.

Then, Aidan's body seemed to expand, to rise up off the bed. He slowly arched his back, pressed his feet into the mattress, twisted his head further to the right and thrust his tongue far out of his mouth. David had the clearest view of his face and chest. He gently placed his hand on Aidan's rib cage and stared intently at his lips, counting the breaths rushing in and out of the his lungs. In half a minute, without a word, David reached for the oxygen mask he had prepared and slipped it over Aidan's curly hair. He looked me squarely in the eyes and said, "This isn't good."

Aidan tightened up and held his breath. A bluish tinge slowly suffused his lips. David grabbed a wide curved plastic tube and, pushing the oxygen mask aside, slid it into the child's trembling mouth. To this he attached a pleated plastic bag, like a small accordion, to pump air into the tube, past Aidan's tongue and into his lungs. I held Aidan's shoulder's, keeping his body steady on the bed so that David could do his work. He pressed the bag deliberately and firmly, forcing air down Aidan's windpipe. I leaned in close to David's hands and could feel the compressions of the life-saving bellows. Time stopped. I was no longer aware of anyone else in the room. Only David and Aidan were there, along with the hissing oxygen and the wheezing bag.

This was a grand mal— "big, bad" in direct translation. In more precise neurological language, it was a generalized convulsive seizure, affecting the entire brain and causing stiffening and jerking of the whole body. While frightening to witness, such a seizure would not necessarily damage the brain, though it may exhaust its victim. The real problem was its duration. If it lasted more than fifteen or twenty minutes we would be facing what the doctors called *status epilepticus*, a persistent and dangerous convulsive state that could permanently harm Aidan. This is what David was working against. He knew that if this was a *status*, compromised breathing might contribute to a very bad outcome.

The physicians' plan called for a hefty dose of intravenous Valium if a seizure lasted more than fifteen minutes. We all knew this, but after about ten minutes David called for the nurse. She did not respond. Maureen went out to find her. Aidan's body was ramrod straight, his muscles hard as wood. Minutes ticked by. I could see through a window into the next room that Maureen was taking charge and preparing the Valium herself. The older nurse appeared next to her, hands moving from face to side and back again in obvious agitation. David called out:

"Get the goddamn Valium in here!"

Maureen rushed back to us with the syringe. The older nurse followed behind in a dither, saying she was not sure what the doctor had ordered or how we should proceed. We told her that, indeed, the Valium was ordered. She hesitated further. David and I worked to get Aidan the oxygen he needed, both of us raising our voices to the nurse, telling her to give him the medicine. She turned one way and then the other, moving about frantically. Finally, Maureen exploded at her, screaming:

"Give it to him now or I will!"

With that, the older nurse took the needle from Maureen, turned to Aidan and began to search for a site to make the injection. His little body was stone rigid, his blood vessels vanishing under his clear smooth skin. She had to find a vein that could hold an intravenous line so that the Valium could be gradually pumped into him. But the seizure was causing all of his vessels to constrict, making it near impossible to place an IV. Hands trembling, she stuck him in the arm but could not insert the tiny filament. She tried again in the other arm, in his foot, his hand. Each time the line blew as the pressure from the convulsion worked against inserting the IV.

By this time, word of our plight had filtered through the hospital, and as people heard that Maureen's little one was in danger, they came to help. A woman from the lab, known for her skill at drawing blood and starting IVs, tried to open a line, to no avail. The nursing supervisor tried. Another nurse gave it a go. Through all of these failed attempts, Aidan's seizure continued unabated. I could barely sense his breathing with my head close by his mouth. David was alternating between pumping the accordion bag and adjusting the oxygen mask in search of the optimum response. In the crowded and tense room, the older nurse disappeared into irrelevance.

A doctor came in. About forty-five minutes had passed since the phenobarbital had been given and the doctor knew that we could waste no more time trying to open an IV line.

He ordered a new shot of Valium, in a concentration and dose appropriate for quick, direct injection. It appeared almost immediately—the work of another, more energetic nurse—and he thrust it resolutely into Aidan's arm. Standing back from the bed, he told us that, most likely, the seizure would interfere with the drug getting into his system, but enough would get through to do some good.

The shot did not stop the *status* but diminished it somewhat. After ten minutes or so, Aidan slowly relaxed his iron tense muscles, settling down into a gentle tremor. His eyes were now fixed straight ahead; his body trembled. An electrical storm was still raging in his brain and we needed to get more Valium into him. We needed an IV line. The pediatrician called a surgeon to come and do a "cut down," an incision into Aidan's body to make way for an IV. It was an unusual step but a necessary one in light of previous failures.

It would take some time for the surgeon to arrive. Aidan's respirations had improved; the initial shot of Valium had eased the terrible tension of the grand mal. The frightening blueness had left his lips. David put away the breathing bag but kept the oxygen mask near Aidan's face, allowing a stream of the invisible mist to curl into his nose and mouth. The immediate crisis had abated, though we still desperately needed to stop the convulsions.

We decided to slip out to call Dr. Graham in Springfield. The doctors had spoken with him earlier, but Maureen and I had not had the chance. He knew better than all the people surrounding us what Aidan was experiencing and what might help him most. We found a telephone in a supply closet and called his paging service. It was dinnertime and he was not on call; we had to wait for him to respond. Maureen and I had not been alone together since the emergency crashed upon us. The small utility room was quiet compared to the clamor by Aidan's bed. Each of us was lost in the demands of the moment. As we stood there among the profusion of medical equipment in the dimly lit space, Maureen sighed deeply and asked, "What should his code status be?"

This was the language nurses used with each other, but I had listened to Maureen and her friends often enough to know what she meant. It was a deadly serious question. Tears welled up in her eyes as she pondered it. A "code" would be called if Aidan's heart stopped beating, but the type of code, or code status, which defined what the doctors would actually do or not do, was our decision. Should we tell them to use all heroic measures to save him, knowing that most of the time such aggressive interventions did not work? Should we prohibit resuscitation? Should we tell them to do some things but not others? We were very close to facing these questions, but we did not have ready answers.

My head was swimming with the implications—we were deciding at what point we would let him die—when the phone rang with Graham's return call. Composing myself as best I could, I recounted for him the past few hours. In a calm, even voice, he reassured me that we would all survive this.

"I have never lost a patient to *status epilepticus*," he intoned confidently.

His opinion was crystal clear: the IV was essential. Once that line was established, a variety of drugs could be used to shut down the seizure, even if it meant something close to general anesthesia. He would make arrangements to have us admitted to the PICU in Springfield as soon as Aidan was stabilized and able to be transported. Then he asked to speak to the local doctors again.

After summoning the pediatrician to the phone, Maureen and I started back toward Aidan's room. Halfway there, I was overcome with hopelessness and grief, my forbearance shattered by the proximity of death. I grabbed Maureen by her shoulders and buried my head in her neck.

"I don't want him to die," I sobbed. "I don't want him to die."

I had stood right there with David, patiently willing Aidan to breathe; I had dispassionately watched his body resist a dozen probing needles; I had coolly conferred with the doctors about what was to be done. But the full realization of Aidan's mortality hit me in that hallway at that moment and I could do nothing else but cry.

Chuang Tzu has a lot to say about death.

This Mighty Mudball of a world burdens us with a body, troubles us with life, eases us with old age, and with death gives us rest. We call our life a blessing, so our death must be a blessing too.

He is not denying the pleasures of life, but just pushing back against those who would exalt those pleasures so as to blind themselves to the inevitable rhythms of existence. By convention, we call life a blessing and, therefore, we fear death. Life, however, has its share of pains and burdens, our bodies eventually rebel against us, and we must recognize that life's good is, of necessity, bound up with its bad. In the same manner, whatever it is that we fear of death must be bound up in its good as well. Chuang Tzu is not a pessimist; he celebrates our physical transformations:

> *We're cast into this human form, and it's such happiness.*
> *This human form knows change but the ten thousand*
> *changes are utterly boundless. Who could calculate the*
> *joys they promise?*

Our bodies are both a burden and a joy; our lives are happy and sad; and our deaths are no different, liberating us from pain and sorrow but stealing us away from familiar pleasures. Chuang Tzu is telling us that once we recognize the give and take of life and death, we can overcome our fears, even the fear of a young child dying in a hospital bed.

> *Birth and death, living and dead, failure and success,*
> *poverty and wealth, honor and dishonor, slander and*
> *praise, hunger and thirst, hot and cold—such are the*
> *transformations of this world, the movements of its*
> *inevitable nature. They keep vanishing into one another*

before our very eyes, day in and day out, but we'll never calibrate what drives them...If you let them move together, at ease and serene, you'll never lose your joy. And if you do this without pause, day in and day out, you'll invest all things with spring.

This is comforting. It places the immediate struggle against sickness and death in a larger perspective, one that transcends our limited form and lifespan. But it is hard to see this, standing in a stark fluorescent hallway just outside the room where your son has almost breathed his last.

The surgeon arrived a short time later. He swept into the room, brimming with a self-assurance bordering on arrogance. When he saw Maureen standing by Aidan's bed, his face dropped, his eyes narrowed. He had worked with her before and recognized her skill and compassion. The pediatrician quickly described our problem and, as he listened, the surgeon took off his jacket and rolled up his sleeves. Looking intently at Maureen, he said, "We'll have this done in no time."

Maureen left the room in search of the various instruments needed for the cut-down. After so many calamities, she decided that she would act as the surgeon's assistant, to make sure, for herself, that it was done properly. Once the tray of materials was assembled, the surgeon folded down the sheet covering Aidan's right foot. He would go in at the ankle, tapping into a major vein running up the leg. He took a scalpel and deftly made a cut just above the foot. Before he could ask for a dressing to wipe away the blood, Maureen was handing it to him. She anticipated his every move and was ready for every turn in the procedure. I marveled at her dexterity. She was in her element, perfectly comfortable working with the doctor. The activity gave her something positive to do; it turned her away from the helplessness of watching Aidan's seizures. She knew very well how to be an accomplished nurse; she did not know—none of us do—how to be the parent of a boy near death.

The cut-down went smoothly and soon a stream of Valium was coursing into Aidan's body, combined with another medication to make sure the *status* was stopped. The mixture was potent. Aidan gradually settled into a deep, drug-induced sleep, his brain, at last, rid of the awful electrochemical monster that had consumed him.

We had to plan quickly for a trip to Springfield. Only one of us could go; the other had to stay with Margaret, now barely two weeks old. Maureen's obstetrician still forbade her to drive because her abdomen was not yet fully healed. She could not bear to be separated from her boy, to let him go all that way without her, especially after the hard work of pulling him through the pneumonia. But she could not make the trip by herself and reluctantly had to agree that I would be the one to go.

There were other pressing matters. We still had not settled on Aidan's code status. We seemed to be safe just now, but none of us knew whether a *status epilepticus* would recur as he was weaned from the drugs. We did not know whether we might face a similar crisis in Springfield. If his heart stopped there, what would we say to the doctors? Maureen had participated in full codes, where all measures were taken to revive a patient: electric paddles; powerful heart medications; ventilators. She had seen people whose hearts were forced to beat and lungs were made to breathe but who died as soon as the machines were shut down. It seemed a futile and inhumane denial of the inevitable. There comes a point, she believed, when the fighting had to end and a person be allowed to die. And we had to come to terms with where that point was for our son.

Of course, as parents, our first impulse was to do all that could be done for our child. He was so young, with so much of his life before him. But we also knew that his brain was so malformed that a prolonged effort to counteract his body's demise could leave him in a coma, or something close to it: a "persistent vegetative state." Every day we struggled to make the most of his limited capabilities, to give him the best life he could have. Trying to artificially prolong that life might actually make it worse for him.

Maureen explained some of the options to me. At one extreme, we could leave word to not resuscitate him at all if he went into respiratory or cardiac arrest. The letters DNR, for "do not resuscitate," would be written in his chart and the doctors would respect our decision. But this was too stark, too fast a surrender. Other, more nuanced, choices were available, variations on the DNR theme. We could tell them not to use the electric paddles to restart his heart, but to do rescue breathing to get him through a prolonged seizure. If his heart stopped, that would be the end of it. If he stopped breathing, we would let them do the kinds of things David had done, but not ventilators, not the machines: they would most likely postpone the final decision to the moment when the plug had to be pulled.

We were moving toward this sort of formulation, a modified DNR, but we were ill at ease with the whole idea of it. It was a God-like role we did not want, determining the minutiae of our son's fate, what would or would not be done as he neared what might be his final moment. If we did not make this determination, however, someone else would, someone who did not know Aidan, who might not be acting in his best interests. To protect his dignity, in either life or death, we had to decide how it would go.

As we were working through these heart-rending choices, the attending pediatrician stopped by to discuss the trip to Springfield. The room was quiet now. Aidan was serenely unconscious. Only one nurse, an attentive and able young woman, hovered about the bed. The doctor asked us to step into an empty room next door so we could have a private talk. He was not Aidan's regular pediatrician but, in a small-town way, he knew of us. A jittery man by nature, he nervously reviewed our case. After a few minutes, Maureen told him of our decision. "He's DNR," she said, and then described the conditions that we attached to that designation. This took the doctor by surprise. He clumsily asked if we understood and were comfortable with that conclusion; we said we understood but could never be comfortable, it was as it had to be. Tears came to his eyes as he fumbled for something to say. It was not clear whether he wanted to commiserate or reprove and the conversation ended on an awkward note.

Before the Springfield ambulance arrived, I went home, threw some things in a bag, kissed little Margaret good-bye and embarked for the all-too-familiar medical center to our south. We had been there with Aidan for other things since that first trip over two years ago. There was a minor surgery; there was a less dire seizure emergency; there were the many, many routine office visits. At this point, I knew the road cold, I could easily find my way there in the dark, in the rain, in the snow. It was easy for me to get there before the ambulance and be waiting in the PICU as they trundled Aidan into the unit.

They set him up in a bed toward the front of the large room, close by the nurses' station. I settled into a rocking chair next to him. Maureen had told me to carry a picture of Aidan and Margaret. It was their first photo together, Margaret tucked in by her brother's side in his crib. I slipped it into a clear plastic frame and set it on top of the IV pump, where everyone would see it. My purpose was not just to display my fatherly pride, but also to remind all of Aidan's caregivers that he was more than a recovering *status epilepticus*: he was a brother, a family member, a person embedded in a complex web of loving relationships.

I spent a comfortless night in the rocking chair. Maureen arrived fairly early the next morning, conveyed by a friend. When she had gone home the night before, she found that a group of my colleagues, who already heard that Aidan was going to Springfield, had organized themselves to drive her back and forth to the medical center for a week or however long they were needed. They knew she was not supposed to drive and they quite willingly did it for her.

We were in the unit for two days. The Valium had done the job of eliminating the seizures but left him groggy and spiritless. He did not try to kick his legs and laugh, nor did he call out for us with his signature "Ah...." His eyes did not shine. We worried that the *status epilepticus*, which had lasted so long and hit him so hard, might have done some serious damage to his brain. Graham said it was possible, but we would not know for some time: in Aidan's case, the short-term effects of exhaustion and weakness could take a week or two to clear up. He was not in any serious danger, however, and they moved us out onto the pediatric floor on the third day.

Because of his lassitude, he was being fed through a tube that ran down his nose and into his stomach. I hated this. Eating was one of his favorite things and the tube separated him from it. I understood why it was necessary but I vowed to fight against it and get him back on his bottle and baby food as soon as I could.

One morning, while Maureen and I shifted about Aidan's room, Dr. Rudi came in. A pediatric pulmonologist specializing in children's breathing problems, he walked with the unbalanced gait of cerebral palsy. His speech was slurred and took some getting used to, but he was obviously a capable and compassionate doctor. He had reviewed Aidan's charts, noticing, no doubt, the modified DNR code status. After some back and forth on the events of the past few days, he asked about our decision. He was the first person to do so; we had told our home-town pediatrician our thoughts on the matter, but no one had raised it with us since. Rudi, though, was intent on pressing us, on discovering if we had contemplated all the possibilities. He listened closely to our rationale. Seeming to accept our approach to cardiac arrest, he was less persuaded by our aversion to ventilators. The machines could be very effective as a temporary tool in treating severe pneumonias and seizures. The concern in his eyes told us that he wanted to make sure that we did not give up too quickly on Aidan. This was clearly important to him. Perhaps, given his own disability, he remembered that someone had once not given up on him.

We told him that we would consider his suggestions but, again, the conversation was unnerving. As he shuffled out of the room, I could feel myself shaking. I did not know why: fear, anger, fatigue. Whatever it was, I knew we had to work out the details of Aidan's code status, to avoid an even worse encounter down the road. Later on, we took Rudi's advice and revised our request and allowed the use of ventilators for the treatment of pneumonia and seizures.

Aidan remained lethargic and his feeding problems persisted. I tried to give him a bottle of formula, but he sputtered and coughed as his weak esophageal muscles let some of the liquid spill into his lungs. A vicious circle was tightening around us. If I could not get enough calories in him by mouth, they would continue the tube feedings, which, in turn would satisfy his appetite, taking away his desire for the bottle. The doctors would then press for a permanent stomach tube, inserted directly into his belly, if Aidan did not resume his normal eating habits. They said that "these kids," severely disabled children, often had eating problems and eventually a tube of some sort was necessary. I utterly rejected this idea. We would not lightly sacrifice his joy of food, his sense of taste. A simplistic assertion of the problems of "these kids" was not enough for me to accept the loss of his gastronomic pleasures.

I fought back, lying to the nurses about how much food went in through the naso-gastric tube and trying to make up the difference with his bottle. In struggling to impress one doctor, I felt like I was performing a bizarre puppet show. Aidan was propped on my knee, curled into the crook of my arm; we sat in a metal folding chair in the middle of the sterile white and gray hospital room. The doctor sat in an identical chair facing us about fifteen feet away. He asked a series of questions, probing Aidan's condition and scribbling notes. I smilingly answered, all the while holding an eight-ounce baby bottle in my boy's mouth, slowly moving it back and forth against his palate to stimulate his sucking response. Everything in my body language was designed to telegraph the message that we were just fine, he was taking his bottle with no problem, we could go home without the damn tube in his nose.

It didn't work. My lies and subterfuge were contradicted by the cold hard numbers on the nurse's chart. Aidan was not getting enough nourishment by mouth. We would have to keep the tube in place for some time longer. Perhaps I should not have made it into such a battle; maybe I should have accepted it from the start as an unpleasant and, with luck, transitory effect of that pernicious and persistent grand mal. But I had made the naso-gastric tube into a symbol of my effectiveness as his father. If I could not nurture him back to regular food, I had failed him. It was a defeat, one of many, that I would have to learn to live with because the next day, after a fortnight in the hospital, they told us we could go home, but the tube had to stay in his nose.

The tube came out a week or so later as Aidan slowly regained enough muscle control to keep himself from choking on his food. But he was not himself. The *status epilepticus* had clearly hurt him. He stopped his kicking—in bed, in the tub, in his blue chair—that he had enjoyed so much. Our call-and-response game ceased. He did not gently coo for our attention and wait for our reply but only silently absorbed his surroundings. The seizure had stilled him.

He lost other skills as well. Before the prolonged grand mal, he liked to play in the baby jumper. It was an odd-looking contraption that hung in a doorway: a long slender spring attached to a little seat, allowing a toddler, one not quite ready to walk, to happily bounce up and down and swing to and fro. The idea was to develop leg strength and balance, precursors to walking. Aidan never progressed to standing and striding, but he was able to use his kicking ability to hop and twist in the jumper. At two years of age he was obviously too big for it and we had to make some adjustments to support him in the flimsy harness seat. When properly positioned, he would push down with his legs and throw himself about with great abandon. Sometimes, when he was in particularly good form, he would heave up his shoulders, straighten out his back, and even hold up his head, bearing his weight on his own two legs. This was one of our developmental milestones and we cherished the times he cheerfully bobbed around in the living room portal.

The *status* ended all this. He could not make his body move as he had before; the strength was gone from his legs and back. His will was deflated, his motivation subdued.

The seizures were worse, too. Before the big, bad one, they had all but stopped, controlled by a single new drug. But afterward they returned and would never be completely suppressed again. The *status epilepticus* had rewired his brain, changed the circuitry so that the once-effective medication was now useless. The neurological changes were, of course, the underlying cause of his other setbacks. Whatever happened to his brain, it had conspicuously narrowed the range of his already modest abilities.

This was hard to take. From the onset of Aidan's condition, we had been robbed of the usual parental rewards, the marvelous surprises and delights children bring. We had yet to come fully to terms with this after two years. We still struggled to recognize Aidan's abilities and make them into our own little victories, however humble they were compared to the developmental norm. His calls, his eating, his kicking: these were the thin straws we grasped, the signs of Aidan's positive growth. They were his links to the world, the points at which he engaged his physical and human environment, and the avenues through which the world penetrated his sightless, speechless realm. They were the foundation of our hope and they were crumbling around us.

At first, we sought to blame someone, anyone, for this unhappy turn of events. Maureen was convinced that the older nurse, whose hesitation made it virtually impossible to start an IV, bore a certain responsibility. If the Valium had reached him sooner, if other drugs could have been introduced on time, perhaps the seizure could have been broken more quickly with less brain damage. I wrote a letter to the hospital administration pointing out these failings, without mentioning her by name, an effort that had no discernible effect on the nurse's career. Retribution was not our purpose in any case. Nothing could bring back Aidan's lost skills. We were wrestling with hypotheticals, the roads not taken that might have yielded a better result. Perhaps the local doctors were at fault for not having a more effective plan or being there to implement it. Maybe we had been derelict in our parental duties. Had we let this happen to him? Were we the authors of his misfortune?

The search for guilt, which so easily turned back upon us, solved nothing, and I gradually gave it up. I came to believe that no one was ultimately to blame. Mistakes were made, but the more fundamental fact was the original reality: Aidan's brain was profoundly malformed, predisposed to these kinds of disasters. If it had not happened that day in that manner, it could very well have happened on another day in a somewhat different form.

Chuang Tzu helped me here.

He tells a story of four men who forge a friendship on the mutual recognition that life and death, and all the transformations of moving from one to another, are simply fleeting moments of the all-encompassing and timeless Way. They laugh together, unafraid of inevitable physical demise. Then, one of the men is felled by a disfiguring illness:

> . . . *a crooked hump sticking out of my back, vital organs bulging over, chin tucked up into belly, shoulders topping skull, nape pointed at sky.*

Obviously, his abilities are in decline. He is losing—as was Aidan—bodily functions that make for human fulfillment. His life is closing in around him. One of his friends ask him if he is resentful. "*No, why should I resent it?*" he replies:

If my left arm's transformed into a rooster, I'll just go looking for night's end. If my right arm's transformed into a crossbow, I'll just go looking for owls to roast. And if my butt's transformed into a pair of wheels and my spirit's transformed into a horse, I'll just ride away! I'd never need a cart again!

This is more than simple and sad resignation; it is irreverent transcendence. He will not only make the most out of whatever his final moments leave him, but he will do it with wit and merriment. And he does this not by simply settling for whatever happiness his predicament offers, but by reaching beyond the immediate emotional possibilities and inventing meanings of his own. *I'll just go looking for owls to roast*: the very absurdity of the thought is liberating. The movement here is from acceptance to freedom.

This life we're given comes in its own season and then follows its vanishing away. If you're at ease in your season, if you can dwell in its vanishing, joy and sorrow never touch you. This is what the ancients called getting free.

I could see it now...Aidan's crisis had liberated me in a way. We had come close to death, had looked over the edge of the precipice, and then moved back. He would die at some point, perhaps young, maybe very young. He was profoundly disabled, even more so than he had been before. But his near-death had altered my vision. The length of his life or the physical particulars of his life were not as important as the mere fact of his life itself. He was following along in his own season, moving on the currents of the Way. Sorrow or happiness were simply beside the point. Of course, my emotions would sometimes bubble up. But what mattered more was making new meanings of his life, ones that did not depend upon my feelings but grew out of the marvels of his experience.

I could feel myself starting to get free.

5.

Being the Child

She stirred from her nap in the small reclining seat, her round, nearly hairless baby head shifting from left to right. The piercing blue of her eyes shone as the sleep fell away. Drawing her hands up to her face, she broke into a beaming smile as she recognized us, her parents, standing around her. She kicked her legs and chattered in her baby-babble precursor to speech. The dog, a massive heft of brown Labrador, five times her size, swished past, making her squeal in delight as she reached to pet the wagging tail. Then, both arms stretched up to her mother, she demanded, in her own way, to be picked up. Margaret was awake.

She was a fairly ordinary baby and brought to us all the usual delights of infancy. But her normalcy was, for us, magnified into marvelous originality. It was our first time experiencing typical child development, even though we were second-time parents. She did everything Aidan did not: she focused intently on everything around her, absorbing the myriad details of daily life; she rolled over from back to front and back again; she held up her head and embraced the world around her. Although her vivaciousness was a constant reminder of Aidan's inactivity, the comparison did not sadden us. She gave us something new and positive, something to leaven the melancholy of Aidan's disability. Her brightness lit up the house and all of us in it. We sang silly ditties to her; we held her up and bounced her about; we peek-a-booed to her and she to us. When we eased her next to Aidan in his crib, she contentedly nestled up to him, comforted by his warmth.

There were questions, however, a whole series of new uncertainties. How would her life with him affect her as she grew up? Would she come to terms with his limitations? Or would she grow to resent him? How would she react if he did, indeed, die as young as some of the doctors believed he would? Could she learn to love him? These were still remote issues—she was only an infant herself—but they skirted through our minds as we watched her grow and thrive

Whatever the nagging long-term questions, Margaret gave new life to the family. Instead of always wondering what had gone wrong for Aidan, we could watch all that was going right for Margaret. This was a boost not only for Maureen and me, but also for our parents.

They had all done their best to be strong for us as we were battered by one disappointment after another with Aidan. Maureen's parents had sturdy exteriors, hardened by the rough and tumble of New York City, where they each had deep family roots. When hardship came, you were supposed to tough it out; don't give on that you were hurting;

don't let others know you were vulnerable. And that was how they handled Aidan's afflictions. That day I rushed home from the hospital to intercept them as they arrived to see their first grandchild for the first time, they silently listened as I recounted an abbreviated version of Aidan's first trip to the PICU. They did not say much; silence tells many tales in their family. They did not ask many questions but simply took in the news and went off to their room to absorb it. There were no public tears, no emotional outbursts; just sad faces and pursed lips.

They went back to the PICU with me the next day and showered their grandson with attention. Their smiles were strong and wide as I took their pictures holding him for the first time, with the black cord of the breathing monitor visibly running out of the baby's shirt. They kept up a good front and soldiered through it. The complexity of Aidan's condition was bewildering to them and they were not confident enough to question medical authorities, but they knew something of life with incapacitated children. Maureen's cousin, her father's brother's son, had suffered a traumatic brain injury and was physically and mentally disabled. It was, to Maureen's parents, a sad and grim thing: the boy's parents struggled mightily to make a life for their child and it ground them down, especially the mother. Maureen's father and mother had seen this and they no doubt had that in their mind as they visited with Aidan in the PICU. So, while they could muster their smiles, they understood this as a sad and grim thing.

My mother asked questions. Reading was the main activity in my family: my mother had been a librarian, my father an advertising executive turned college professor, and my sister a voracious consumer of science fiction. I was the least literate of the crowd. When I had to tell her of Aidan's misfortune, my mother commiserated, and then questioned. She wanted to know if he would walk and talk and see. For years after, she would query, "Will he get better?" And my response was always, "I don't know," or "probably not." She wanted to be hopeful, to keep open some possibility of resolution, to turn the tragic story toward some happier ending. But the plot proved impenetrable to improvement.

My father had died before Aidan's birth, which might have been just as well. He was emotionally weak and drank for strength. He used to call alcohol his "armor"; it was the stuff that steeled him against life's daily defeats. He drank to fend off his insecurities and anxieties, and to hasten his own demise, knowing full well that the booze and the cigarettes and the fatty diet all increased his chances for a heart attack. And that was precisely how he went: a sudden, massive coronary at sixty-two, the year before Aidan was born. Had he lived, I can only imagine that the stress and sadness would have pushed him further into the bottle.

As it turned out, we were fortunate with how the three remaining grandparents related to Aidan and us. The Christmas before Margaret was born, Aidan's third time through the season, we made the grand tour of family sites. The drive to Maureen's parents in Staten Island took us right through the northern suburbs of New York City, where my mother lived. Stopping first at her house, we spent the better part of a day there. After lunch and opening presents, Maureen stretched Aidan out on the living room rug. Kicking happily—he had not yet had the *status epilepticus* that set him back developmentally—he drew my mother down on the floor with him. She stayed next to him, tickling his chest and matching each of his delighted laughs. She obviously loved him.

There was much the same feeling when we arrived in Staten Island. Maureen's parents and their neighbors had an annoying habit of referring to "poor Aidan"—"How is poor Aidan today?" "Isn't poor Aidan a blessing!"—which we countered as best we could. But this linguistic peek into their deeper feelings did not keep them from making for him the happiest Christmas they could. His favorite foods were on the table: squash and beets and pudding. Santa Claus came with fitting gifts. There were musical toys to enhance Aidan's best sense, hearing; other playthings with tactile surfaces to stimulate his touch; no baseball mitts nor tricycles. The older generation had some knowledge of what he could not do, and they made their choices carefully and lovingly.

We had heard stories from other parents of disabled children about how their parents furiously denied the hard reality of impaired grandchildren and retreated into combative self-pity. One angry grandmother, unable to affirm the fullness of an incomplete baby, had gone so far as to stop talking to her daughter. Our parents did not make such new problems for us. They struggled as we did, searching for the best interpretation of what was happening to us all, but they did so in ways that recognized and supported Aidan as a member of the family.

Margaret made all this easier. One smile, one clap of her tiny hands and the awkward silences and intrusive questions about Aidan were forgotten. She did not cause us to ignore Aidan; she simply provided a respite from the sadness he could inspire. Maureen's parents proudly paraded her around their tight-knit neighborhood, finding happy words to tell the world of their beautiful granddaughter. Beside "poor Aidan," there was now "dear Margaret." Instead of rare medical conditions and gloomy predictions, we now had before us the look and sound and play of a typical baby. My mother did not have to ask unanswerable questions about this little girl: her vigor and beauty and potential were there for all to see.

It was getting harder to hold my academic career together. As an analyst of Chinese politics, I had to go to China regularly, to stay close to its fast-changing society, to see it and hear it and feel it. At the very least, I needed access to large research universities, where I could get my hands on relevant newspapers and journals and books. My remote little corner of western Massachusetts was not well-suited to serious study of contemporary China. The college's library could not support all of the Chinese language materials needed to stay on top of events. The World Wide Web had not yet exploded on the scene. To do the kind of scholarship and writing required to keep advancing in my field, I had to go to China or to China research centers. Or I had to let that part of my life go.

The sabbatical to Australia and Japan, which would have placed me in some very good places to study China, had to be cancelled. It had taken me some time to face and accept this reality. I had held out until June, when Aidan was eight months old and it was readily apparent that his brain was significantly malformed, before I formally notified the various schools that we would not be coming. The head of the department in Australia was nice about it. He wrote back that he, too, had a child with serious health issues and could empathize with me. He held out the possibility of another trip sometime in the future when things looked up. It was hard to see when that might be.

So, instead of Canberra and Kyoto, I found myself holed up in an odd little office in the basement of the college chapel, a last-minute arrangement that gave me a place to write whatever I could. Freed from my teaching duties for the year, I had to publish or perish. The next year I would be up for a tenure review, a process which would determine whether I would be given a permanent position or be turned out into the unpromising and unforgiving job market. To succeed, I had to publish articles in academic journals. I had already published one book and another edited textbook, so I was in a fairly strong position. But my college, and especially my department, prided itself on demanding a great deal of its junior, untenured members. They were always looking for more, always asking what had I accomplished lately. One of my senior colleagues had already let me know that he thought my published work, as a whole, was rather weak. My scholarship was, as he put it, "occasionistic." What he meant by this awkward term was that my various publications ranged over a wide variety of unrelated topics and questions; they did not come together as a coherent body of work. With this sort of tortured criticism, I had to assume my job was not safe.

Losing this job would be a disaster. Not only was the pay good and my hours flexible, allowing me to make trips to the many doctors and therapists we frequented, but, most important of all, the medical insurance was strong. We were becoming a very expensive case, and we would have our share of run-ins with callous HMO functionaries, but since the college was a preferred customer, there was never any threat of losing our coverage. Once we even changed from one plan to another, and Aidan's diverse problems could not be counted as "preexisting conditions." But this would last only as long as the job did. I had to get tenure.

Crammed in my cellar refuge, I wrote about what I had seen during our last long stay in China three years earlier, in the spring of 1989. The massive popular protests that had swept through Beijing then, filling Tiananmen Square with thousands and thousands of people and ending so tragically with the massacre of hundreds, had also burst upon the city where we were living at the time, Nanjing. I had watched from the very first day in April. Most of my students, Chinese graduate students from all over the country, were swept up into the passion and promise—though a couple of them became informers for the in-house Communist Party committee. I had sat in trees and climbed telephone poles to photograph and chronicle the sea of humanity as it flowed through the streets in May. I had held up my hand in the "V" sign, the universal signal of support for the students and their victory. And I had wandered through the city in June, sadly witnessing the end of the movement in the aftermath of the killings in Beijing. Nobody died in Nanjing, but several of my new friends were arrested.

I wrote about what I had seen then, but I had to squeeze the life out of it to make it analytic and objective for an academic audience. I did it and published it in a respectable journal. But I could never be sure what would be enough for tenure. I wrote another article for another journal and planned others. The book project I proposed was critically torn apart by my senior colleagues. I just kept working: the medical insurance was too important to lose.

It was impolitic to talk about Aidan's trials with the senior members of my department who would be rendering judgment on whether I would keep my job. They expected me to reach a certain level of professional achievement whatever the circumstances; the fact that I had family problems was immaterial. They were not mean to me, but neither were they overly sympathetic. I never raised Aidan with them; I only talked about him if they asked and I always limited how far I would go in any such conversations. On one occasion, a senior colleague inquired about Aidan's health. I allowed myself to tell him that Aidan, in the days just after his birth, had come close to death. He replied that, given the severity of Aidan's condition, and its effects on Maureen and me, it might "be better" if he did die. He meant this as a consolation. I did not respond but turned the conversation in another direction. Later, alone, I was dumbfounded by his insensitivity. How could he possibly think that I could believe it would "be better" if Aidan died? I could think of ten thousand other ways that it could "be better," far short of his death. This man was not a parent himself, and I realized that he had no inkling of the ferocity of a parent's love.

As it turned out, I did get tenure. On the day they told me, I did not shout for joy. I expected this outcome: it would have been surprising if it had gone the other way. Rather than an explosion of happiness, my feelings ran more toward a great sigh of relief. It had been uncertain and now it was settled. I would keep my job. I did not have that to worry about. Maureen was six months pregnant with Margaret and we would not have to move.

In the afterglow of Margaret's birth, as she grew and thrived and strengthened us all, I found a chance to go back to China for a short trip. I was overseeing a program that sent a couple of our graduates to China each year to teach English. They went to Guangzhou and Hong Kong, places where I had done research in the past, places that I knew and liked. It seemed a good idea for me to go and talk over various elements of our affiliation with administrators in both cities. The college picked up the tab. Maureen's parents came up from New York to help out with the kids. Aidan was stable and out of danger. So, I flew off to Hong Kong and Guangzhou.

It was an uneventful trip but still satisfying. I could not do any serious researched, just talked with my counterparts by day and wandered around the cities at night, lapping up the atmosphere. Guangzhou was most interesting. It had been five years since I was last there, but the city had changed noticeably. The road to the best university now sported a Pizza Hut, a MacDonald's, and a Kentucky Fried Chicken. Sleepy old one-story buildings, gracefully mildewing in the humid air, were being knocked down by the block to make way for towering steel and glass shopping malls. Guangzhou was the center of the fastest growing region of China, which at that time was the fastest growing region of the world economy.

One evening I ambled through a night market, surveying the many wares for sale. Old women beseeched me to buy their fruit, a young man beguiled me with counterfeit Rolex watches. The air was filled with the fried oil smell of innumerable roadside cooking stalls. My thoughts ran to my career. How could I find a way to spend longer periods of time in China, doing the kind of research needed for academic work? I could not imagine bringing Aidan here. I could not see how I could just leave Maureen for weeks or months to bear the burdens of his care by herself. The sing-song sound of spoken Cantonese swirled through my ears. I walked and walked, turning the heads of a cluster of adolescent girls, giggling at the sight of a lone foreigner. Young men hung on the street corners or read the dozens of posters advertising job openings. I watched them as they searched for new opportunities, new lives, and they watched me as I searched for mine.

Aidan got sick that winter. He came down with pneumonia again, and we acted quickly to get him to the big medical center in Springfield. We needed aggressive treatment of the pneumonia itself, to shut down the fever, to reduce the chances of another prolonged neurological crisis. Maureen could not abide our small-town hospital: she sill held the older nurse there responsible for Aidan's developmental regression. The road to Springfield became more and more familiar to us.

We again met Dr. Rudi, the pulmonary specialist with cerebral palsy who had counseled us on Aidan's code status. He had told us then about the most drastic treatments for pneumonia, slowing respirations to such an extent that a ventilator might be necessary to keep a patient breathing. This was obviously not the first choice for action, but we knew that, if need be, he could push the limits in attacking the fluid in Aidan's lung. Through his slurred speech he made clear to us that he was very capable of the most resolute doctoring.

One of the first steps to be taken, however, was rather old-fashioned. The respiratory therapists would come around every six or eight hours, depending upon the severity of the pneumonia, and roll Aidan onto his side. With a cupped hand they then stoutly pounded his back over his lungs. Working up and down his back, they would settle into a steady rhythm, a lively drumming, to drive the bad stuff from his airways. When one side was done, they turned Aidan over and pummeled the other. This was Chest Percussive Therapy—CPT—and it seemed like an ancient impulse. *Thump, thump, thump, thump*: a brisk 4/4 meter of the hollow thud of rounded hand on flat back, the background tom-tom of pediatric pulmonary. *Thump, thump, thump, thump.* If I closed my eyes, I could sense a jungle somewhere, aboriginal people dancing and chanting to their drums, all helping the shaman cure the fevered child.

However primitive it appeared, the CPT worked. Before the treatment, Aidan would be straining for air, rasping and wheezing as he worked to pull oxygen through his congested lungs. By the time the respiratory therapist left, his chest was moving evenly and easily up and down.

They did not rely solely on the back clapping. Usually they started with a medicated mist, a drug that would float up his nose and down into his chest and open up the clogged passages. This "up-draft," followed by vigorous CPT, induced Aidan to cough, moving the congestion out of his lungs. If he was in greater distress, the therapists would intervene more directly. Slipping a thin plastic tube in his nose and fishing it into his bronchial tubes, they suctioned out the

mucus. The powerful air compressor used to create a vac-
uum rattled loudly and shook the wall and the head of the
bed. The suction tube hissed menacingly. It was obviously
uncomfortable for Aidan. The therapists said it was like
having the wind knocked out of him. All the air in his lung
was sucked out immediately, leaving him gasping for breath
and fighting the slippery plastic demon in his nose. But it
pulled out the sinister phlegm and brought him, ultimately,
to comfort.

We were three days in the hospital this time around. It
was, for us, a relatively relaxed stay: no seizures, no PICU,
no near-death. They sent us home with new training and
equipment. We learned how to do CPT, so we could inter-
cede immediately should we face pneumonia again. From
our local medical supply dealer, we rented a suction machine
to perform, when needed, that unpleasant task. We also
bought a smaller air compressor which we could use to give
him up-draft treatments. His room became a miniature
pneumonia ward.

All these preparations were well taken. About a month
later, Aidan came down with pneumonia again. We did not
go to Springfield for this spell, though neither did we return
to our little local hospital. Instead we went to a medium-
sized medical center in the county seat, about half an hour
away. One of the pediatricians there was truly remarkable
with a stethoscope. She held it to Aidan's small chest, shifting the cold metal device back and forth, listening intently.
Using only her ears she was able to pinpoint precisely where

the clogged spot was in his right lung. An X-ray later veri-
fied her stunning accuracy. It was reassuring to watch such a
skilled doctor at work, but we did not stay in the hospital for
long. After two nights they sent us home, knowing that it
was not a severe case and that we were well-equipped to
carry out the needed treatments ourselves.

A few weeks later, it happened again. We seemed to be
settling into a disturbing pattern of regular pulmonary infection, a winter of pneumonic discontent. One time was serious
enough to see us back in Springfield, watching at Aidan's
beside while Dr. Rudi oversaw a treatment to reverse the
pressure in his lungs, to open them wider, to dislodge the
menace.

Questions were now being posed regarding the causes of
the chronic recurrences. Perhaps, some doctors speculated,
his low muscle tone was making it difficult for Aidan to routinely cough and clear minor congestions that then developed into more dangerous infections. These physicians were
unsurprised by this possibility: it was common, they said, for
"these sorts of kids" to have pulmonary problems. Their
quick categorization of Aidan as one of "these sorts of kids"
irked Maureen and me. They were too quick to embrace an
easy, formulaic answer, too distracted to press on to see if
there was some more unique etiology here. Was there some
other connection between Aidan's unusual neurological condition and his propensity for pneumonia? Too many doctors
were uninspired by such questions; they were too busy to
look beyond facile stereotypes.

Dr. Rudi did not accept the easy response about "these sorts of kids." He pressed on, ordering more and more tests, more than we really wanted. With his cerebral palsy placing him among "these sorts" of people, he more readily looked on Aidan as an individual. It was Dr. Rudi who started to wonder whether the pneumonias were being caused by food, coming up from the stomach or down from the mouth, getting in Aidan's lungs. There might be a gastroenterological cause of the pulmonary problem. He ordered more tests: scopes that looked down Aidan's throat and scans that peered into his stomach. For one examination, we had to hold Aidan and feed him his bottle while an ultrasound video was taken of this esophagus, to see if liquid was slipping into his lungs while he drank. When they played the recording back we could plainly see that this was indeed the case. On the ghostly white and gray screen, through the outlines of muscles and organs, small drops of his formula could clearly be seen trickling past his trachea. Such tiny dribbles and specks of food became hosts for infection. Aidan's daily meals were, in due course, stealing his breath.

There was a more remote neurological basis for this new problem. Aidan's malformed brain was the basis of his generalized low muscle tone. All of his muscles, throughout his entire body, were soft and loose. Even his epiglottis, the small flap of cartilage that keeps food from sliding into the lungs, was lax, allowing for aspiration pneumonias.

This diagnosis provided some relief. At least we had a more precise understanding of what was happening; now something could be done to counteract the problem. But as we began to consider just what we should do, relief gave way to deeper disappointment. To keep food from going down his trachea, the esophagus would have to be by-passed. A feeding tube running into his stomach was recommended, a permanent little line poking from his belly, forever taking away the pleasure of taste and texture of food. Another irrevocable step away from normality, another unsettling shift toward aberrancy.

By the time we had worked through the many illnesses and tests, winter was giving way to spring. However, the cold was not abating. We felt it deep inside us as we pondered the possibility of a feeding tube. We knew of other parents who, when faced with this decision, rejected the tube. They saw it as unacceptably unnatural, an extreme measure that denied something fundamentally human: the capacities to chew and taste and swallow. It blurred the line between healthy life and the PICU. Tubes were for hospitals and sick beds, not for the everyday family dinner table. We felt these misgivings, too. For us, though, there was an inexorable logic at work. At three and a half years of age, Aidan could not feed himself; he would never feed himself. While he reveled in certain foods, he could not tell us what he wanted. He was wholly dependent on us to discern his preferences, blend his meals, spoon his mouthfuls. The tube seemed simply an extension of these already prevalent dependencies—at the sad cost of taste. Now, with food-induced pneumonia, which was worse: a life with taste and potentially deadly pulmonary infection, or a life with unappetizing formula running through a stomach tube and safe, comfortable breathing? We dejectedly chose the latter.

The hard choices did not end there, however. What kind of procedure should he have? What would the medical side effects be? The gastrointestinal specialists said that a tube going directly into his stomach, piercing his abdomen just above the navel, by itself would not settle the issue. Aidan's low muscle tone also weakened the seal where the esophagus met the stomach, and that would allow formula to push back up his throat and spill into his lungs. A bottom-up aspiration would replace the top-down one. They said surgery would be needed to tighten down the entryway into the stomach.

Maureen was dead set against this. She knew that this was a significant operation, with risks of infection or other complications. I was uncertain. With no medical background to judge the best course of action, I was less willing to reject surgery out of hand. My hesitancy made me useless to Maureen's crusade to save Aidan from the knife. In the end, she prevailed. She found a surgeon who agreed that other steps could be taken before the more involved intervention. It was a heroic effort on her part, but it had pushed us apart for several weeks. I had not actively resisted her, but my doubt was a difference between us. Time gradually filled the rift as we went on and attended to daily necessities. The accumulation of many small, common activities helped us overcome the occasional major disagreement.

When all was said and done, Aidan had a gastrojejunal feeding tube. It went into his belly, like a stomach tube, but then ran down into his small intestine. The formula we gave him was unlikely to reverse back through the constricted passages at both the bottom and the top of the stomach, reducing the risk of aspiration. Only a minor puncture through his belly was required, no major surgery. It was a somewhat unusual arrangement but, from the sunny summer day when all of this was finally worked out, the pneumonias stopped.

It had taken eight or nine months to move from the first autumn pneumonia to the final July g-j tube. We were worn down by many hospital stays, uncertain diagnoses, tense conflicts with doctors. And in the end we had to accept another loss for Aidan. No longer would he be able to suck his bottle, filling his belly and calming himself with the rhythmic tug of cheeks and tongue. No longer would he smack his lips as we spooned in dollop after dollop of strained carrots or beets or chicken. No longer would whole bowls of chocolate pudding and whipped cream disappear under his chin. We could give him little tastes once in a while, but we could not risk pneumonia, and its attendant seizure-generating fever, for even a modest amount of food by mouth.

Aidan's life was all about him and us letting go of expectations and desires. We had to let go, continually, of whatever image of him we held in our minds. As the typical became the impossible, we had to redefine his normal, our normal. It was now normal for us to run food into his small intestine by either a portable pump or a large syringe. Seizures were normal: they still happened many times every day in various forms. We knew how to distinguish the onset of a major neurological explosion from the run-of-the-mill seizure; it was routine for us. Not walking, not talking, not seeing—all of this was our unexceptional everyday experience. Of course, at times it could be deeply unsettling. Sorrow could easily arise if we dwelt too long on what a normal life might have been for him. With no real choice, however, we had to take normal for what it actually was. We had to let go of the ideal child.

I had to let go of some elements of my professional life as well. Just after the first pneumonia had hit that fall, I had been invited to attend a two-week seminar in Beijing. It sounded great. Fifteen or so academics from all over the U.S., with varying backgrounds in international relations, would meet with a range of officials from the Chinese government. For me, it would provide new contacts and new sources on Beijing politics, and it would put me on the streets of the capital to witness another slice of China's transformation. In terms of my working life, the opportunity came at a perfect time. I needed to develop a new body of research, the basis for another book. Not knowing how Aidan's health might change, and confident that my absence would not be too much of a burden for Maureen, I signed up for the trip.

It was not to be. I was supposed to go in June, just after we had confronted the likelihood of a feeding tube for Aidan. Maureen and I were struggling to understand pediatric gastroenterology and the causes of pneumonia; we were disagreeing over the merits of stomach surgery; we were swirling in a torrent of new tensions. It was obvious that I could not up and leave at such a moment. My letter declining the option was short and direct.

While it may have appeared to my in-laws and non-academic friends like an unjustifiable luxury, to me the Beijing trip represented professional growth and progress. Without it, I was cut off from my vocation. How could I study and write about Chinese politics if I could not go there? And, without that sort of access, what could I accomplish in small-town Massachusetts? Not much, it seemed to me. To be sure, with tenure, I was safely ensconced in my job. They would not fire me if I slowly faded from relevance among Sinologists. There were plenty of "deadwood" academics filling offices in small colleges across America, protected from unemployment by lifetime tenure, quietly ossifying intellectually with less and less to say that anyone, their students included, really cared to hear. As I let go of the Beijing trip, this was my image of my own future.

China was slipping further away; Aidan was losing ground. Central features of my life were collapsing before my eyes. There was nothing I could do but let go and watch and wonder what would come next. Anger was futile; it changed nothing. Regret went unrequited. I had been here already and my emotions were now less raw but I still could not easily resign myself to what seemed to be inevitable frustration.

And then there was Margaret. She was happily oblivious to my struggle with disappointment. Free from the burdens of adult expectations, she was enthralled by her daily discoveries of the world around her. The most mundane objects—a piece of ribbon, a shiny spoon—inspired her most joyful laughs. Beyond her basic needs of food and physical comfort, she did not have to go very far for contentment. There was nothing extraordinary about her in this regard. She was just being a baby, with the usual baby desires and enjoyments, but her baby-ness was informing my adulthood.

I remembered, and went back to find, a passage in the *Tao Te Ching*:

One who embraces the fullness of Virtue,
Can be compared to a newborn babe.
Wasps and scorpions, snakes and vipers do not sting
    him;
Birds of prey and fierce beasts do not seize him;
His bones and muscles are weak and pliant, yet his
    grasp is firm...

"Virtue" (the *Te* of the *Tao Te Ching*—sometimes translated as "integrity") here means the recognition that every entity in the universe is complete and integral unto itself. Each thing has its own particular character, its unique disposition. We cannot use one thing to assess another; rather, we must look to see how each thing expresses itself and fulfills its own possibility. This is what the infant does: she observes and absorbs, she does not categorize and judge. She innately understands that each thing and every person, even a severely disabled brother, has its place in the world and its own particular value. From this vantage point, she is safe from the wasps and vipers of disappointment.

An infant, then, when compared to most adults, is closer to an appreciation of the complex totality of the Way, which is, after all, the agglomeration of all things. Chuang Tzu extends this idea a step further:

> In all beneath heaven there's nothing bigger than the tip of an autumn hair, and Tai Mountain is tiny. No one lives longer than a child who dies young, and the seven-hundred-year-old Peng Tsu died an infant.

Even the oldest man—Peng Tsu is a mythical Methuselah-like figure—has no advantage over the youngest child in knowing the Way, because all there is to be known can be grasped by the naïve wisdom of the infant. Letting go of desires, so hard for adults, is easy for the child who has not yet spun a web of assumptions and plans. The baby sees the integrity, or virtue, of each thing she encounters in and of itself. We think long life brings us a better understanding of the world, but in the end, *no one lives longer than a child who dies young.*

Perhaps, then, a child suspended in permanent infancy, like Aidan, was not quite as disabled as we thought.

The question for us adults, searching as we were for a transcendent meaning of our worst tribulations, was this: can we learn to be the child?

Winter solstice was near and the cold December darkness had come early that Friday evening. Aidan had already gone through two pneumonias and we could not know how many might lie ahead, nor that a tube would be poking into his stomach in six months time. For this night, he was comfortably resting in his crib. Maureen was at work at the college infirmary, as she was every Friday night while school was in session. I was home with the kids. Margaret was sitting on the living room floor, opposite me across a black and white blanket that looked like the skin of a large Holstein dairy cow. It was about seven o'clock.

Margaret was sitting up, a skill she had mastered in the past few weeks. With only ten months behind her, she was a bit wobbly as she stretched her arms out to her sides and then brought her hands together in an exaggerated clap. She clapped and wobbled, clapped and wobbled. Then she planted her hands down on the floor in front herself, using them to steady her little body. As she shifted her weight forward, she found a way to tuck her legs under and kneel. Looking like a sprinter positioning herself in the starting blocks in preparation for the big race, she gently rocked back and forth on hands and knees. Her head rose and her eyes fixed on me, a smile of recognition spreading across her round face.

Slowly and deliberately she slid her right hand forward, hesitated for a moment and then shuffled her right knee behind it. As she sensed her body out of balance, with her right side pushed ahead of her left, she quickly picked up her other hand and moved it forward, the left knee following instinctively. After an unsteady pause on all fours, she repeated the maneuver: right hand forward, left knee, left hand, right knee. With each successive round, her movements became more fluid, though still somewhat tentative. Arcing slightly to the left, she crawled across the living room floor, across the silly cow blanket, right to where I was sitting.

As she moved, my heart quickened. By the time she arrived in my arms, a warm elation was washing over me.

"You crawled," I sang out, "you crawled right to me!"

She could sense my happiness, and smiled and clapped in return. I quickly turned her around and scurried to the other side of the room, encouraging her to repeat her performance in the other direction, which she did at once. I hooted and hollered with joy. I had never seen a child discover mobility.

When Maureen came home, at about midnight, Margaret was already in bed asleep. Before she could put down her bag, I was breathlessly recounting Margaret's triumph. We hugged and laughed and cried and cried.

6.

The Human Realm

The three pennies clattered down on the table before me: heads, heads, heads; nine, a pure yang line. The next toss yielded tails, tails, and heads, which added up to seven, another yang line, though not pure this time; then, another seven. The fourth toss was an eight, followed by two sixes, both pure yin lines. The image thus created was "Peace," or "Tranquillity," the eleventh hexagram of the *Book of Changes*.

The question was: how would Aidan fare in his move to pre-kindergarten at the local elementary school? He was just turning three years old, eight months past the terrible *status* and two months before the first of the chronic pneumonias that would lead to the g-j tube. And his fortune was decidedly mixed.

The sense conveyed by "Tranquillity" was one of balance and harmony. The great primal forces—yin and yang—were equally poised in the hexagram: three solid yang lines on the bottom and three broken yin lines on top. At a moment of such complementarity of light and dark, strength and submission, good things were bound to happen;

hence, the oracle stated: *the small departs / the great approaches.* Good fortune was the general prediction. I had images of a happy group of children surrounding Aidan with friendship and fun; he would be the yin to their yang. But when I looked more carefully at the commentaries associated with the pure yang and yin lines, something more troubling appeared. While the first two—the first yang and the fifth yin—reinforced the overall positive message, the last, the sixth yin, issued a warning. Rather vaguely, the text read:

> *The wall falls back into the moat.*
> *Use no army now.*
> *Make your commands known within your own town.*
> *Perseverance brings humiliation.*

The harmony of the present moment was bound to slip away as time unfolded and change occurred. The solid wall of good fortune that now surrounded us would decay and tumble into a moat of stress and strain. The martial metaphors suggested avoiding bold action and sweeping expectations; they implied that we should keep our own counsel and not try to fight when things went wrong. I knew that Maureen was not likely to follow this advice. When things went badly for Aidan, when people were not doing for him what she thought they should, she would fight back resolutely. I would just have to follow along and watch to see if such perseverance did, indeed, bring us humiliation. So, while there was much good to be found in these passages from the *Book of Changes*, it was with a certain foreboding that I accompanied Aidan and Maureen to his first day of preschool.

The classroom was a good size, filled with furniture and toys. Two long, low shelves—one filled with books, the other with blocks—partially divided the space; a wide gap between them allowed for movement from one end of the room to the other. Half of the floor was covered with dark gray institutional carpeting, the other half with pale yellow linoleum. All of the chairs and tables were low to the ground, perfect for a three- or four-year-old, a long way down for an adult. The walls were adorned with instructive artwork and pictures: a train, with each car noting the birthday of a child in the class; an oversized calendar, to help the preschoolers keep track of time and weather and holidays. The doorways were rather narrow and we were not sure if Aidan's wheelchair would fit. Indeed, our worries ran much deeper, to how well Aidan would fit into the commotion of public school.

We recognized some of the parents, dropping off their little ones on the first day, and some of the kids, who had crossed paths with Aidan at one public event or another. There were about fifteen children there. Two others had "issues"—Attention Deficit Disorder and the like—and one child's disability was similar to Aidan's: he could not see, talk, or walk, and was significantly mentally retarded. The rest of the class, the majority, was made up of typical children, bouncy and bright three- and four-year-olds. This -

pre-kindergarten, named "Side by Side," was specifically designed to integrate kids with disabilities, whether mild or severe, with their average peers. The teacher was certified in special education. She knew how to create an environment that included all the children together. Aidan would be part of the class. He had his own place marker on the carpet for circle time, when they sang and shared stories and news. It seemed a supportive and harmonious setting.

Aidan had been in social services programs before. By law, all children with diagnosed disabilities are entitled to therapies and care that will maximize their developmental potential. From birth to age three, these sorts of benefits are usually provided through Early Intervention agencies. This had been the channel that brought Linda, the African-American physical therapist, to Aidan's aid. Other specialists had also been assigned to our case: an occupational therapist, who concentrated on Aidan's fine motor development, especially his fingers and hands; a vision therapist, with an extraordinary bag of visual tricks; developmental educators, who engaged him cognitively and socially. Many of these encounters happened in the security of our home. When Aidan was about a year old, we enrolled him in a day program in a nearby town. Instead of many different therapists working individually in many separate houses, all of the various services were centralized in a single location. Children congregated together, adding a social dimension to their treatments; therapists moved efficiently from child to child; and we met parents in similar circumstances. It was all very flexible and cooperative.

In Massachusetts, when a disabled child turns three, responsibility for therapy and care shifts to the local school district, a completely different world. However welcoming the teacher was that first day, she was embedded in a more structured bureaucracy. Unlike Early Intervention, which was created especially for children with developmental delays, the elementary school served the interests of the entire community, the most gifted students along with the most severely disabled, the average and the extraordinary. The Side by Side pre-kindergarten was somewhat sheltered from the raucous competition for resources and attention that pervaded all public education: it paid for itself through tuition charged to the typical children who attended. But we had already felt the sharp edge of financial constraint.

At our first meeting with the school administration to create an Individualized Educational Plan (IEP), the official document that defined what kinds of therapies Aidan would receive, the superintendent, who doubled as director of Special Education, revealed his budgetary concerns. When the physical therapist suggested that she work with him "two or three" hours a week, the superintendent was quick in response:

"Good, we'll do two hours a week, then."

He straightaway went for the minimum. No one tried to counter him. Maureen and I did not know what was possible or usual, so we too kept quiet. We had grown to trust the Early Intervention administrators, who seemed driven primarily by what would be best for Aidan. However, the cash-strapped public education system would be more of a struggle, however. Aidan would be just one more line item vying for scarce expenditures. We would have to negotiate and wrangle for his best interests.

Despite the difficulty, there were also new and comforting surprises in Side by Side. The children in the class took to Aidan immediately. At first, there was an explosion of questions:

"Why can't he walk?"

"How come he can't see?"

"Why doesn't he talk?"

However abrupt, this grilling did not grate on us. With their questions, the kids were not trying to place Aidan in a social category, to classify, differentiate, and interpret; they just wanted to know why he could not walk or see or talk. When we answered with something like, "He's just made that way, some people can walk and others can't," they quietly accepted this new information and went about their play. They might ask about other facets of Aidan's life, prefaced by "why"—something we asked ourselves all the time—but straightforward answers, without too much medical detail, sated their curiosity. After a couple of weeks of regular contact, they no longer questioned Aidan's disabilities. He became a given element of their social scene, a classmate, a friend, someone to invite to birthday parties or to share secrets.

School thus provided Aidan with a new social life. It was there that he was surrounded by his peers and given a place in line. At home we could love him and care for him, but we could not, by ourselves, construct a full and rich public identity for him. We alone could not make him all that he could be, not without a broader community. And he seemed to sense this, for it was at school where he was most attentive, brightening his eyes at the clamor of his classmates. The other children were quite happy to be around him. Their abilities were magnified in the mirror of his limitations, so they were pleased to congregate around him. They greeted him in the morning, sometimes bringing over their favorite stuffed animal for him to feel; they sat with him at story time or helped him swirl his hands in finger paint. They made for him a world of sensations and relationships.

It was at school, too, that Aidan had the greatest effect on people around him. In his first year, one of his classmates had a pronounced speech impediment. Ricky's words were often unintelligible, drawing quizzical looks, and sometimes giggles, from his peers. As a result he shied away from speaking, a reaction that could worsen his problem. The teachers and therapists did a good job in engaging him and supporting his efforts to shape his mouth and tongue to produce recognizable English. But he was very much aware of his idiosyncrasy and uncomfortable with it. In Aidan, however, he had a friend, one who did not strain to understand his words or laugh when they came out garbled. Aidan did not judge or correct. He just sat silently, varying little in his countenance whatever Ricky might say. On more than one occasion when I was in the classroom I noticed Ricky close to Aidan, happily chatting away, gaining the practice he needed to clarify his speech, sustained by the presence of an uncritical buddy. Aidan was yin to his yang, and was able to help.

Chuang Tzu tells a story of a man who had his foot cut off, most likely as punishment for some crime. This in itself is an eye-catching image in Chinese literature: an incomplete man, a deformed body. For Confucius, the great ancient Chinese upholder of filial duty and social hierarchy and proper ritual, physical wholeness was of the utmost importance. From a Confucian perspective, it would be terribly offensive to one's ancestors to die with a deficient or desecrated body. Chuang Tzu thus takes aim squarely at Confucian rectitude when he turns the tables in this short fable, and puts Confucius himself in the position of praising the one-footed misfit.

It seems that one of Confucius's disciples comes to him one day to report that the mangled man has taken up teaching and is attracting as many adherents as the venerable philosopher himself. To this, Confucius surprisingly—this is Chuang Tzu's mischief at work, after all—responds that, clearly, this man is a "master, a sage." The disciple is puzzled; how can it be that this obviously imperfect man commands the respect of the upright and wise, and physically whole, Confucius?

The key to the man's insight, Confucius says, is his transcendence of worldly concerns. The mutilated one does not let life or death affect his outlook and takes unforeseen surprises in stride. His teaching is literally wordless: he does not say anything to the multitude surrounding him, but simply radiates a certain wisdom. Seeing the integrity of each thing unto itself—even those things that appear imperfect and damaged—he does not have to make distinctions and judgments, but can perceive the totality of the Way, where all things move as one and the same.

> *Seen in terms of sameness, the ten thousand things are all one. If you understand this, you forget how eye and ear could love this and hate that. Then the mind wanders the accord of Integrity. And if you see the identity of things, you see there can be no loss. So it is that he saw nothing more in a lost foot than a clump of dirt tossed aside.*

With the serenity that comes from knowing there can be no loss, the hobbled man becomes a sought-after teacher. People flock around him to learn how they, too, can detach themselves from their desires and escape from their frustrations. It is his tranquillity that draws their attention. We are hopelessly battered by the daily tumult of our responsibilities, pushed and pulled to such an extent that we lose track of who we are. So, we look to the calm and collected man, seemingly disabled, who is at peace with his world and himself. And we look to him because:

> *A man...cannot see himself in running water, but in still water. For only what is itself still can instill stillness into others.*

Aidan is still. He sits, wordlessly, in his wheelchair, his happy little friends around him, unconcerned with distinctions and differences. Has he moved beyond worries of life and death? We can't know; yet perhaps Chuang Tzu is right: *there can be no loss.*

But I was still restless. Aidan missed a fair amount of school that first year as we battled pneumonias and confronted the feeding tube. Springtime was consumed by doctor's appointments and hospital stays. A great deal of my time was taken up with one medical problem or another. It was hard to keep up with my teaching, and writing was next to impossible. I had cancelled the Beijing trip and felt increasingly isolated from China and Chinese politics. Whatever I was learning from Aidan's wisdom, I was still immersed in the rushing water of contemporary American life, where frenetic productivity, as opposed to sedentary tranquillity, is the measure of success. Insecurity and self-doubt were creeping into my psyche.

And then something started to unfold that would bring East Asian politics right into my small New England town and catapult Aidan into the middle of an international controversy.

In the late Spring, as Aidan's first year in pre-kindergarten was drawing to a close and we contemplated a g-j tube, my college announced that they would grant an honorary degree to the prime minister of Singapore, who had studied economics here many years ago. The president of the college had mentioned this decision to me earlier, and, at first, I tepidly supported the idea. I knew that Singapore was infamous for its draconian social control and engineering—fining people for chewing gum, putting TV monitors in public toilets—and I was aware that it was then in the news for the caning of an American teenager who had been caught spray-painting graffiti on parked cars. More importantly, I was also aware of how the ruling party there used libel laws and a compliant judiciary to cement its hold on power, making a mockery of its ostensible democratic parliamentary system. It was somewhat disconcerting to associate our college with this mean little city-state, but on the other hand, we were a rather parochial institution. Any connection, even a ceremonial one, to the wider world, and Asia in particular, might be a good thing.

After the formal announcement of the planned degree, however, I started to change my mind. I spoke with another faculty member who was outraged by the idea and he inspired me to read more, to look more carefully at Singaporean politics. I learned that, under their Internal Security Act, a person could be detained indefinitely and without legal recourse on the flimsiest of "national security" charges. Eight years earlier, in 1987, twenty-two people, mainly religious social workers and members of a left-wing theater group, were rounded up and accused of fomenting a "Marxist conspiracy." The man who was now Prime Minister, Mr. Goh Chok Tong, whom the college wanted to honor, had overseen this action on his way up to the top political post. Even more disturbing was the systematic repression of academic freedom in Singapore. I found numerous cases of teachers and writers being harassed by the government or losing their jobs for putting forth ideas that deviated even slightly from the preferred party line. It became more and more obvious to me that we should not honor Mr. Goh, the leader of a political system that contradicted essential principles of American academia.

I emailed the president of the college and told him of my newfound concerns. He demurred. The trustees of the college had already extended the invitation and it would be disrespectful, at this late point, to rescind the honor. The college's good name was now on the line. I countered that the public embarrassment which would ensue from paying tribute to an authoritarian leader would do even more damage to the school's credibility. He politely disagreed and the decision stood.

Several other faculty members were starting to pull together to try do something to withdraw the promised degree, which was scheduled to be ceremonially bestowed early in the following fall semester. We wrote to the trustees, to no avail. We surveyed the faculty and discovered that most were uncomfortable with the plan, but the president was unmoved. The degree would be granted, he told us.

We had exhausted our local options for action. The spring semester was ending, students and faculty would soon be leaving for the summer, and the momentum of the cause was ebbing. So, we decided to go public, to approach national newspapers with the story in hopes of creating a minor media storm, shaming the trustees into reversing course. The *New York Times* was on the top of our contact list. We knew that a couple of columnists there had written critically about Singapore in the past, and we sent short notes to them outlining our situation.

It came as some surprise, however, when I heard back from William Safire in early July with news that he was planning a column on our efforts to stop the degree. He interviewed me over the telephone; I gave him background on our plans. By that time, we had invited a number of prominent opponents of the Singaporean ruling party to make presentations and we were ready to ask the prime minister to meet his most formidable critics. It was this counter-award ceremony that Safire highlighted in his biting *New York Times* op-ed, "Honoring Repression." Hoping to connect with sympathetic alumni who might be able to pressure the college president and trustees, I also asked Safire to print my email address, which he did.

The response was immediate and overwhelming. The day after the piece ran, my email inbox was flooded with messages from infuriated Singaporeans. As it turned out, the tiny republic was one of the most wired places in the world, and people there were proud and ready to strike back against any foreign detractor. I also heard from dissidents, from Singapore and around the world, who shared with me their stories of the repressive power of the government. It was an instant and tumultuous immersion into Singaporean politics.

All of this was unexpected. I had to change my daily routine to respond to the deluge of messages I was receiving, especially those from kindred spirits willing to bolster my position. I posted regularly on the largest electronic bulletin board for Singaporean issues, parrying the assaults of the youth wing of the ruling party and other irate nationalists. I became the *bête-noire* of the Lion City.

The conflict escalated bizarrely a few days later. My home telephone rang at about six in the morning while I was still asleep. I groggily answered and a reporter from the *Straits Times*, Singapore's main newspaper, crisply asked me to respond to a front page story they were running that day on prime minister Goh's invitation to Safire and me to come to Singapore, at their government's expense, to debate the prime minister at their leading national university. I asked her to repeat what she had just said; I was sure that my sleep-addled mind had not comprehended accurately. She said, again, in lilting Singaporean English, that I had been invited by the Prime Minister to debate with him. I told her that this was the first I had heard of it and I was not ready to reply formally.

My head was spinning. I had just been challenged to debate a prime minister! They would fly me there and put me up and televise a face-to-face exchange with their top national leader. There was some obvious risk in all of this. The arguments I had been making, especially about the debased Singaporean judiciary, were most definitely actionable there. If I repeated these indictments in an auditorium jammed full of screaming government supporters, I would not only be shouted off the stage, but could quite possibly be charged with libel or worse. But they would probably not arrest me because that would simply make my point for me. If I went knowing I would technically lose the debate—the audience would certainly be against me—there might be ways I could win by publicly advancing the forbidden arguments. And it would be immensely entertaining!

When I got to my office that morning, there was a telephone message from Safire's office. I called him back and we chatted.

"So, what should we do?" he asked.

I chuckled to myself. Here "we" were, leading conservative-libertarian columnist and typical left-liberal academician, accidental allies thrown together by a fortuitous political turn. He said he would certainly turn down the offer, viewing it as a political stunt designed to embarrass him publicly. I told him that I was still thinking about it, that I might actually do it, even though they would be spoiling for my failure. He ended by telling me to be on the watch for his next column.

That evening, Maureen eyed me suspiciously across the dinner table as I recounted how I was being drawn into the vortex of Singaporean national life. Her steely gray gaze was prologue to her definite response:

"You're not going, are you?"

She did not have to elaborate. Aidan's feeding tube was less than a month in operation, too soon to know for sure if it would break the succession of pneumonias. Even if arrest was a remote possibility, how could I even contemplate heightening the stress on our household with a political fantasy in Singapore? She did not have to say any of this; I knew it already, deep in my heart. I was only slightly disappointed, however, preoccupied as I was with the frenzy of the political battle.

After Safire's next column, a caustic and hilarious rejection of the prime minister's poisoned apple, I told the *Straits Times*, which had taken to calling me daily, that I could not travel to Singapore because family responsibilities would not allow it, but that I still wanted to debate Mr. Goh, perhaps through a real-time video conference. The reporter pressed me for details. What sort of family commitments? I hesitated. I did not want Aidan's disabilities to be splashed across the newspapers, for him to be known internationally only for what he could not do. All I said was that my son had been ill of late. A few days later, the story ran in the *Straits Times* under the headline: "Crane wants a debate—even without Safire." They dutifully reported: "As his son's illness made it difficult for him to leave home at this time, he suggested that the debate take place through a teleconference."

In this manner Aidan had been introduced to the prime minister of Singapore. I was imagining the scene in the Mr. Goh's office. Ensconced in parliamentary splendor, cabinet ministers and trusted advisors were considering what to do now that they had learned Crane's son was ill and that he would not be coming to Singapore. Were they debating whether the "illness" was real or not? Did they appreciate the irony of my invoking family obligations, a revered Confucian principle, to frustrate them, who self-righteously proclaimed their rectitude as Confucian gentlemen? Whatever they were thinking, for that day, Aidan was on the top of their agenda. Not bad for a boy, not yet four years old, who could not see or talk or walk.

There were recriminations. Editorialists and letter writers in the *Straits Times* castigated me as a fraud and a coward. On the electronic bulletin boards, the youthful defenders of Singaporean honor pressed back at me:

Crane cited "family commitments" as a reason for his decision. For someone who has gone out of his way to make such a big fuss about the whole affair, his reason does sound quite lame to me....After all, he is (I assume) a serious academician, is he not? Is he adverse to collecting more information and engaging in more discussions?...I think he owes us a good explanation.

I did not take the bait. Aidan would not be fodder for their assaults. I retreated—a Taoist impulse—and fought my battles at times and in places of my own choosing. The Prime Minister did not take up my offer of a teleconference, which would not offer him sufficient political advantage.

The degree ceremony went forward as planned and we had a number of speeches and demonstrations, calling attention to the suppression of free inquiry and expression in Singapore. It was a grand time. For three days running, the back room of a local restaurant was crammed with leading Singaporean opposition politicians and dissidents. We talked and drank and I learned more about politics there than I ever could have imagined. If I could not go to China, having Singapore come to small-town Massachusetts was the next best thing. The prime minister's retinue was large and well-oiled, keeping up a steady stream of criticism and invective. In one event, the prime minister solemnly warned a full auditorium not to listen to George Crane: "He has not been to Singapore."

And so I hadn't. In one sense, we lost: Mr. Goh was given his honorary sheepskin. But we made our point about the incongruity of the award; and in making so much noise, we demonstrated by our actions the freedoms that Singaporean academics were daily denied.

We were still stymied by Aidan's seizures. As he approached his fourth birthday, we had tried about ten different anti-convulsant medications. Only one of them had made a real difference but, after a seizure-free two months or so, the big *status epilepticus* had reversed that effect. Since then, we lived with fitful interruptions of Aidan's comfort.

His seizures came in many forms. "Epilepsy" proved to be a fairly meaningless term to describe the wide variety of jerks and shakes and faints. Physicians used a much more diverse vocabulary to categorize and diagnose seizures. A primary distinction was between "partial" seizures, which were focused on a specific part of the cerebrum, and "generalized" seizures, which seemed to explode across the entire brain all at once. Effects were further classified into two broad types: "simple" seizures that did not impair consciousness, and "complex" seizures that involved some sort of blackout. Since generalized seizures usually altered consciousness in some way, the three main types of seizures the doctors discussed were generalized, simple partial, and complex partial. Things got increasingly complicated as more particular effects and manifestations were taken into account.

Aidan appeared to have generalized seizures, though some partial complex episodes were possible as well. Myoclonic jerks, which forced him to fold into himself with knees up and arms in, were common. These occasionally happened in a series of ten or fifteen jolts in a row. He would sometimes have atonic, or "drop," seizures, in which most of the major muscles of his body suddenly went limp. If he had been able to stand, he would have crashed instantly to the floor. As it was, he simply drooped into his wheelchair or wilted into our arms. At other times, his body shook all over in the most familiar image of a seizure; this was a tonic-clonic episode, when muscles would rapidly contract and relax, contract and relax, rattling him remorselessly. Most disturbing were those spasms that stopped his breathing. These apnea-inducing occurrences were most often associated with absence seizures, when the mind just goes blank. His eyes would open wide and stare straight ahead as his head twisted to the left and his lips slowly turned blue. He usually came out of it in a minute or so, but it was always a disquieting reminder of that very first seizure when he was nine days old.

Perhaps the most bizarre neurological outbursts were his laughing seizures. With these, he pushed back hard against his chair, stretched his arms and turned his head slightly left. Then, his mouth opened into a toothy smile and he let out a loud and hearty laugh. It all lasted only about a minute or so. When it first happened, we were not sure what it was. He looked so happy! It had to be sheer joy just brimming over. People around him smiled and remarked on his mirth. Its repetition, however, raised our suspicions, and we came to learn of gelastic seizures, when his malfunctioning brain produced a laugh-like convulsion, rather than real merriment. It seemed the electrical tempests in his head were so insidious we could not even trust that his happiness was genuine.

The various sorts of seizures would come and go, mix and match, of their own accord. For a few months, it was a combination of absence-apnea seizures and myoclonic jerks. That would fade and a new pattern of, say, mild tonic-clonics and gelastics would emerge for a period. They had lives of their own, seemingly resistant to the many drugs we used in a vain effort to suppress them. We tried just about everything: harsh-tasting phenobarbital by mouth, crushed Klonopin tablets by feeding tube, powerful steroids by injection. We even went to a Chinese herbalist, who gave us a paper sack full of sticks and leaves which, when boiled, produced a musky and gritty liquid that Aidan, in the days when he still took food by mouth, could not abide. Nothing really worked.

I did not, therefore, have high expectations when we tried a new antiseizure treatment as the Singapore flap subsided in the cool autumn just before Aidan turned four. This was a dietary regimen—hopefully more palatable than the Chinese herbs. It would be made easier by the fact that everything went directly into his small intestine through his feeding tube, rendering the question of taste largely irrelevant. Known as the ketogenic diet, it was based on observations made long ago by doctors that fasting had helped some people control their seizures. When food was withheld for a day or two, the body would begin to metabolize its own protein, leaving noticeable amounts of organic compounds called ketones in the blood-stream. If a high-fat, low-protein and low-carbohydrate diet was then resumed, high levels of ketones remained in the system and, for some, seizures dissipated. Nobody knew precisely why the ketones might be connected with neurological improvement, but it seemed to work for a good number of people in dire need. Since we had tried just about everything else available, we figured that we should give this a go.

Aidan had to be admitted to the hospital and closely observed for two or three days. They would monitor the initial fasting and ensure that his metabolism went into ketosis, the production of ketones, and that we got started on the diet properly. It was another trip down the well-worn path to Springfield. Maureen stayed in the room with him—one of us always stayed in the room with him when we were in the hospital—and I shuttled back and forth from home. Margaret, now twenty months old, accompanied me one day and, toddling on her own, she was quite a hit on the floor, wandering unsteadily along the hallways, the pointer and index fingers of her right hand wedged in her mouth.

When we returned home on the diet, we had to follow a very precise routine. Every day we carefully measured exact portions of an oily white liquid, microlipid, concocting a high-fat formula that included a small scoop of a powdered carbohydrate. Aidan received a fixed volume each day, supplemented by additional water. We had to be very careful not to give him anything else in his tube or in his mouth that might contain more carbohydrates or proteins. Toothpastes, cough syrups, vitamins, and the like, all had to be examined to make sure they did not contain glucose, which could shift his metabolism out of ketosis and possibly spark a seizure.

After a few weeks, we noticed that the number and severity of his seizures seemed to be decreasing. We had never kept an exact tally of his daily brain activity; it was too depressing to note the hour-by-hour accumulation of tremors and convulsions. It was more of a general impression of improvement that we were sensing. The promise here was that, with enough progress with the diet, we might be able to back off the powerful drugs that made him groggy and glazed. Maureen, with her wariness toward chemically-dependent conventional medicine, was particularly hopeful that a less harsh but still effective treatment might be found.

She wanted her boy's mind to be as clear as possible to take in what he could of the world around him.

But we seemed to have traded one problem for another. Aidan became more and more uncomfortable as the diet advanced. The high-fat content was irritating his digestion, even his stomach. This gastric activity was, in turn, sending acidic fluid up his esophagus, the painful reflux—or "heartburn"—that the gastrointestinal doctors had long predicted. His aide at school, a splendidly observant woman with a nursing background who worked with him every day, was noting in her daily log more and more crying and complaining. We tried Zantac, a strong anti-reflux medicine. Yet still he sobbed. His nights were increasingly disrupted by painful outbursts; all of us were losing sleep, becoming more irritable and brusque. A further threat was aspiration pneumonia, if the reflux went high enough to spill into his lungs. Then we would be facing the up-draft and the CPT and the suction machine and maybe the hospital. As the stomach problems worsened, it was harder to see the neurological gains.

We had to quit the diet and return to yet another synthetic prescription. The seizures continued, ebbing and flowing by their own devilish dynamic. We had reached for a better result but could not grasp it.

Chuang Tzu buzzed in my head. Maybe the problem was not our lack of success with the diet; maybe we were trying to do something that simply was not to be done. We wanted to stop his seizures with as few side-effects as possible. We wanted to push against what seemed like a natural abomination, the random electrical jolts in his brain. But maybe there was no way to overcome the seizures completely; maybe we simply had to live with marginally effective drugs at modest doses that would not totally stupefy him. Maybe that was his way, a way we had to follow, not fight.

If you know what is beyond your control, if you know it follows its own inevitable nature and you live at peace—that is Integrity perfected. Children and ministers inevitably find that much is beyond them. But if you forget about yourself and always do what circumstances require of you, there's no time to cherish life and despise death. Then, you do what you can, and whatever happens is fine.

Late fall was giving way to winter. The sharp, crisp air carried a faint scent of smoke, the residue of decaying leaves and grass and flowers. Frost settled from the morning cold and the last ranks of southbound geese honked their sad seasonal farewells.

Margaret was getting steadier on her feet. She traipsed around the house in her miniature shoes, happily reaching for the cat's tail or the low kitchen drawers at her eye level. This day she was bundled up against the chilly autumn temperatures, which had penetrated the not-yet-winterized house. Her brightly colored wool sweater was slightly too large, rounding her dimensions to a pleasant plumpness.

Two fingers perched in mouth as usual, she turned into the living room and found her brother there. Aidan, also warmly dressed in a thick cotton sweatsuit, was folded into a beanbag chair on the floor. He sat there still and silent, free, for the time being, from the seizures that regularly unsettled him.

Margaret fixed her eyes on him and took her tiny steps across the room to his side. She looked back at me for a brief instant and then turned and faced her brother. Quite of her own accord, with no prompting from me or Maureen, she took her fingers out of her mouth, stretched her arms wide, leaned forward, and embraced him. She rested her cheek against his, lovingly holding the hug for a long and wordless moment.

Every morning, before taking him into the social world of school, I wash Aidan. We do this while he is still in bed, lying straight on his back. Starting with his face, I slip my left hand under his head to steady it and speak to him, alerting him to the coming shock of dampness on his brow. Even with my spoken introduction, the first swipes of the warm washcloth invariably startle him. He widens his eyes in reaction to the wet assault. I carefully rub under and behind his ears, working toward his eyes to cleanse away the sleep from their inner corners. Soap comes next, soap on cheeks and forehead and chin, soap to dissolve the dirt from his smooth skin.

I move down to his chest and abdomen. Here the soap comes first, rubbed across the front of his torso. My fingers find their way to the small tube protruding from his belly. I deliberately wash the ring of skin surrounding the plastic, aware of the microscopic possibilities of infection. There is no sign of redness or contamination there; the daily ablution does the trick. Reaching my left hand across him and under his left shoulder blade, I roll him onto his right side, facing me, and scrub his back. Then, I shift him onto his back again and undo his diaper. He is still in diapers, he will always be in diapers.

I draw back the foreskin of his small, uncircumcised penis and rub the warm soapy washrag there. He twitches at the touch. Maureen had been adamant that he not be circumcised. She had witnessed the cutting of other boys and saw no good reason to inflict such pain on her son. I am agnostic on the issue of circumcision and her preference has prevailed. It has left me with this particular chore, an odd reversal of the Confucian demand that the son unfailingly serve the father: here I am daily doing this most intimate work for my eldest male child, the carrier of my family name.

Rolling him on his side again, I scrub his buttocks and down the back of his legs. His left knee, resting above his right, moves forward and I have to brace his body against the gravity pulling it prone. Gently but decisively, with the dexterity that comes from performing an everyday task, I push him onto his back once more. He is clean and ready to be dressed.

I am proud of his cleanliness. The tidy site where his feeding tube enters his stomach is my badge of honor. I hear doctors and nurses remark on how the site should never be allowed to get dirty and contaminated. Aidan's is clean and clear; it always is. No one will ever see a shadow of neglect there. I wash him most mornings, and when I am not there, Maureen is. We keep the dirt away from him. And then we send him out into the world.

7.

The Form of
this Body

His second year in Side-by-Side moved along and melted into summer, only to resume again for a third year the next fall, and we fell into a steady routine. Aidan and I were usually the first ones into the pre-kindergarten room in the morning. I liked to get there a bit early, earlier than the teacher wanted, to avoid the rush at the door and in the hallway. We parked by the rear entrance next to where the van pulled in and off-loaded the kids in wheelchairs, the "handicaps" as the older typical kids called them, riding in the "handicap van." We never used the van. When we had first seen it, there was no one other than the driver to look after the children. What if Aidan had an apnea seizure and the driver was unaware of it? To avoid this question, I drove him instead.

We were consistent in our habits. As we pulled up to the door, Aidan, now five years old, was safely strapped in his extra-large car seat, a blue cloth-covered cushion around his neck to hold his head upright. I hopped out of the station wagon and quickly moved around to the rear hatch, pulling out his collapsible wheelchair. It took a minute or two to open up the frame and slide the seat into place, but I was well-versed in the mechanics of the chair—the springs and knobs and levers—and was never too long in getting it ready. Pivoting back to where Aidan sat, I unsnapped his seatbelt and slid my right hand behind him and curled my left under his knees, gently lifting him up and out of the car and into the wheelchair.

The building was awkwardly designed. It had originally been three separate buildings, near one another but disconnected. When the Town rejected the idea, and expense, of a new building in the late 1970s, a second-best renovation plan knit the three structures together by way of a long corridor and a new gymnasium. Our parking spot was behind the Western-most building and Aidan's classroom was in the middle section of the E-shaped edifice. We wheeled our way down the long hallway, lined with large un-insulated windows and always chilly in the cold months. Squeezing through a door and a narrow stairwell, past the library, we turned right, through large double-doors and down the locker-lined corridor of the middle building. The walls were festooned with artwork from the preschool and kindergarten classes: happy blue cows dancing with ragged red lions on yellow lawns and purple mountains. Aidan was confined to the first floor of this part of the school, as there was no elevator to allow him access upstairs.

I stopped by his locker and, when he was bundled up against the weather, slipped off his coat and hat and stowed them behind the narrow metal door marked "Aidan," written in both standard letters and in Braille. His backpack, containing a change of clothes, diapers, and emergency seizure medicine, also went into the locker. The medicine was always close by him, in case danger erupted.

His teacher was usually there when we arrived, though some days we entered the room alone. I sat quietly with him, not wanting to disturb the teacher's morning rituals of preparation, and waited for his aide to arrive. For a child as medically involved as Aidan, the school district was required to provide a teacher's aide, a "one-on-one" in the local parlance, to work exclusively with him. The classroom teacher still ruled the roost, overseeing the general curriculum and daily flow of activities, but the aide had the most sustained and intimate contact with Aidan. We had been careful to request that Aidan's aide have a medical background, a person who would be able to assess and respond to his multiform seizures, someone who could tell the difference between everyday neurological flare-ups and strange new brain dysfunctions. Karen got the assignment and she entered the classroom at precisely the same time every morning.

Karen was a meticulous and careful woman. Trained as a nurse, she had found her way into the elementary school for a less time-consuming job. For all of the emotions that Aidan could inspire, she never let his seizures or crying or fussing shatter her professional calm. Her countenance was always even and unruffled. In the four years she worked with him, I never heard her raise her voice.

When Karen arrived in the morning, we first exchanged small talk, and then I would relay any important bit of information: how Aidan slept the night before; what his seizures were like since he awoke; whether he had a doctor's appointment or other reason to leave school early that day. She always listened to me intently, asking a follow-up question here or there. When I was done but before I left, she turned to the daily journal that she and Maureen kept, writing back and forth to each other on the details of Aidan's days and nights. Karen knew that Maureen followed everything more closely than I; she knew that the mother-nurse at home kept a much more intense focus on her baby than the father-teacher rushing off to work. Only after Karen had reviewed Maureen's notes, and questioned me on whatever might be written there, was I free to leave.

Some days, I lingered awhile and watched Aidan's classmates come trickling into the room. This year, his third in Side-by-Side, Katherine was his alter ego. The bossiest child in the class, Katherine lived up to her regal name by self-assuredly informing all and sundry of what needed to be done. She oversaw morning dress-up, when the children pulled various costumes out of a trunk and modeled for one another; she reminded everyone of their daily duties: who was to lead the line down the hallway, who was to help straighten up the toys, who was to report on the weather. Katherine went about her self-appointed duties with a certain world-weariness, as if she had seen it all before but just had to go through it one more time to make sure the others got it right.

With a heavy sigh, she entered the room, clutching her favorite stuffed animal under her elbow. She proceeded straight to Aidan, greeting him in a loud and clear voice, then taking his hand and running it over the soft fur of her toy tiger, knowing that tactile stimulation was one of the best ways of relating to him. She helped push his wheelchair over to the costume trunk and decide whether he would wear the purple hat or the grass skirt. Or she brought over the toy pizza and played at serving him his favorite flavor. As the teacher called the children into a circle for the day's first organized activity, Katherine would intermittently interject her thoughts on Aidan's preferences:

"Aidan likes to feel the sponge at the water table."

"Aidan should sit with us at lunch."

She knew him well and had knit him snugly into her classroom routine.

At recess, Katherine was right in the thick of the other students as they brought sticks and rocks and grass for Aidan to feel. Some days, after school, I would find all sorts of tiny debris fallen down the sides of his seat cushion, evidence of the children's activity. In the classroom, if Aidan had a seizure and his head fell forward, Katherine, when seated next to him, would calmly and gently push his head upright and continue on with the task at hand, unfazed by the neurological interruption. If he burst out in a laughing seizure, she would roll her eyes knowingly. If he drooled onto the bandana draped around his neck, she would carefully wipe his chin, without disgust or criticism. This was his normal, and it was her normal, too.

Katherine, and most other classmates, were accustomed to his physical configuration. His body, its limitations and abnormalities, were familiar and unthreatening to her. She did not think twice about the centrality of Aidan to her school life. It was a completely accepting sort of thoughtlessness: her attachment to him did not need explanation. He was, without thought or question, without hesitation or doubt, her friend.

A sage inquires into realms beyond time and space, but never talks about them. A sage talks about realms within time and space but never explains. In the Spring and Autumn Annals, where it tells about the ancient emperors, it says the sage explains but never divides. Hence, in difference there's no difference, and in division there is no division. You may ask how this can be. The sage embraces it all. Everyone else divides things, and uses one to reveal the other. Therefore, I say: "Those who divide things cannot see."

(27)

Chuang Tzu would like the pre-kindergarten. He would see the sagely wisdom of Katherine simply going about her business, in no need of explanation or analytic distinctions. It is only as we age that we learn how to create difference, how to separate out the normal from the abnormal, the pretty from the ugly, the smart from the dumb. We weave intricate webs of personal understanding and public policy from the threads of difference and division. But, however useful this kind of categorization might be for science and business and warfare, we miss something when we divide, we miss the whole, we miss the Way.

For Aidan, school simultaneously divides and combines. He is defined as a "severe needs special education" child, a designation that brings certain prerogatives. He is entitled to inclusion in the Side-by-Side program; he is entitled to a one-on-one aide; he is entitled to transportation to school; he is entitled to physical and occupational and vision therapies. It is only the state's prior division of disabled from abled that secures these services for him. In his case, the differences are made strikingly obvious by his wheelchair and his seizures and his speechlessness. But once in the classroom and surrounded by the other children, there is no difference in his difference. Katherine and the other children embrace it all; they do not divide Aidan off into a category of his own and then use that distinction to reveal themselves. They can see Aidan's place in the class, his social value, because they do not divide.

Aidan has a similar effect on the adults that are with him on a daily basis. Karen, through her close daily contact with him, is able to read his moods and desires. She knows his different cries and moans, what he sounds like when he needs a nap or when he is uncomfortable in his wheelchair. And, being a mother herself, as well as a nurse, she knows how to respond when a child, any child, calls out. While she is, no doubt, still steeped in the pervasive categorizing that fuels modern adult life, for brief moments at least, her time with Aidan allows her to see the limits of social distinctions. Aidan brings her closer to the Way, for, as Chuang Tzu says elsewhere: *Where there is Way, boundaries haven't yet begun being.*

The classroom teacher reports much the same effect:

> Aidan contributes very much to the fabric of the class. His quiet ways have enabled his classmates to relate to him and accept him for whom he is. When his peers interact with him, they do so because they are doing something with and for him, not his aide. He has assisted many children in learning to appreciate each other's differences and to understand disabilities.
>
> Thank you for letting me share Aidan's year.

Looking back on it, the crying started in July, in the summer between his third and fourth year in Side-by-Side, when he was three months short of six years old. It was a different sort of cry, not a cry of fatigue or mild discomfort, but a cry of deep and real pain, a cry with tears and writhing. It did not dominate our attention at that time because it was brief. He cried for ten or fifteen minutes, shaking us and making us mentally review what might be wrong—stomach reflux, post-seizure headache, ear infection—but then it subsided on its own accord. It did not return for a couple of weeks.

When it did, however, it was, again, a cry of a different sort. He could not tell us what was causing it, where it hurt, so we continued to search for the source and puzzle over what might be happening. It disappeared once more as fast as it had come, and so passed from our concern.

The outbursts became more frequent and persistent as the summer turned to fall. One day Karen noted in the daily journal that Aidan had to be taken out of class and into the nurse's office because he was crying so hard. We also saw it at home. Following no discernable pattern, he would suddenly tense up and scream, sometimes in the morning, sometimes at night. We could not see how the apparent pain was related to any particular cause. Occasionally, it would come on after a seizure, but not always. It might happen when he was lying down or sitting up; it could come just after he had had some formula in his tube, or much later. Yet week by week, it seemed to be getting worse, with longer intervals of intense distress separated now by days, not weeks.

We did not mention it to his primary doctor until October. Having been through so much already and not wanting to be seen as incapable of managing his care, we had tried desperately to handle the emerging problem ourselves. After all, no one knew him better than we did. The pediatrician, an energetic woman with an office in a larger town about a half hour away, quizzed Maureen at a hastily arranged office visit, during which, of course, Aidan was perfectly serene. She raised the possibility of muscle or bone pain. As a six-year-old boy who never stood or walked on his own, he was bound to have orthopedic problems, however much physical therapy we did. Bone growth was influenced by the pressure and pounding of everyday use; without that daily stimulus, the hip socket, for example, would not fully form around the balled head of the femur, causing slippage and eventual chronic dislocation, a terribly painful condition. Perhaps, she suggested, we were at the leading edge of such a scenario. She ordered higher doses of prescription pain medicine and told us to call her in a week if things got worse.

And worse they did get. The screaming swelled into top-of-his-lungs shrieking. Maureen was at her wits' end. All of her nurse training and motherly instincts were failing Aidan. Her beloved boy was suffering from some terrible, unknown malady and she could not cure him. She had tried everything, searched for any sort of remedy. Staggering into the kitchen one day, exhausted from anxiety and tears, she did not know where to turn next. Margaret, then only three and a half, was there. She was not afraid at the sight of her distraught mother. Seemingly too young to understand what was transpiring, she calmly said, in a voice unusually mature and composed:

"Mommy, it's time to call Dr. Vickie."

Of course. It was the obvious thing to do: call the pediatrician again. It had not come to Maureen's mind at that moment; the mountain of frustration weighing down upon her had obstructed her perception. But Margaret's suggestion, uttered as if she were a close and sympathetic adult, brought Maureen back to action. She called Dr. Vickie who, this time, could hear Aidan's agonized wails in the background and immediately began the process of admitting him to the hospital. Margaret had helped move things along.

In the hospital—the medium-sized facility in the county seat—they ran various tests to discover the underlying cause of the hurt. It was an unsettling few days. Tucked into a small single room, so as not to upset other children with his screams, we struggled to medicate and soothe Aidan's rebellious body. He intermittently lapsed into explosive fits of crying and pain, offset by sheer exhaustion and sleep. From the hours of anxiety, however, eventually came an answer. Dr. Vickie entered on the third afternoon with a report from a sonogram done on Aidan's abdomen. The internists who had reviewed the hazy shadows of his organs had found tiny kidney stones. This was both unusual and clarifying: odd in that six-year-olds rarely turn up with kidney stones; instructive in that kidney stones are known to be excruciatingly painful. We could now add urology, along with neurology and gastroenterology, to the list of Aidan's ailments.

All was not quite that sure, however. The sonogram report stated that the stones were still "high up" in the kidneys. Usually stones bring pain as they pass out of the kidneys and down the narrow ureters and into the bladder. The doctors were puzzled that these stones would cause the kind of agony that Aidan was experiencing. Nonetheless, they decided it was best to seek further expert attention, and we prepared for yet another trek to Springfield.

We descended into darkness. That early November, as we arrived in Springfield, the air still had the temperate feel of autumn; when we finally returned home, after Thanksgiving, winter had crashed down upon us, hard and sharp, with cold ice-edges cutting deep into our hearts.

The question about the location of the stones loomed large for the doctors in Springfield. The attending pediatrician, an oddly aloof and chilly woman devoid of the usual openness and affability of a children's doctor, was quick to embrace the theory that the stones were not causing the pain. Her blank face was impervious to Aidan's screams, and she did not alter her countenance as Maureen and I pressed her to treat the stones. Instead, she ordered moderate levels of pain medicine and consulted with other specialists.

Graham, our neurologist, was called in and, true to his calling, he thought neurologically. He wondered if Aidan's apparent discomfort was really a reaction to his seizure medication. Maureen and I doubted this; we had seen such side-effects before and they were nowhere near as severe as what Aidan was now expressing. Graham further speculated that some sort of "neurological decline" was the cause. If more abnormalities had developed in Aidan's brain, strange behavior might result. We were skeptical. Aidan was, to us, obviously in pain; his terrible screeching and thrashing about was coming on more frequently and lasting longer and longer. He needed more aggressive pain treatment, now. Graham ordered an MRI of his brain, and the house pediatrician stuck to her wait-and-see attitude.

The idea that was infusing the minds of the various doctors involved—the attending pediatrician, Graham, the residents, other specialists who came and went—was that this was not really pain at all. It simply looked like pain and sounded like pain, but was actually a bizarre neurological event. They gave us pitiful looks: the poor parents who think that their son is in real pain, not able to understand it isn't what it appears; how awful for them to have to go through this. But all we wanted was morphine.

Maureen knew something of pain and pain management. Years before, she had worked in a cancer unit in a major hospital in Washington, D.C. Having seen a good deal of suffering there, she cursed the hesitancy of some doctors to prescribe sufficient amounts of pain medication to ease the agony. Now we found ourselves in similar straights with Aidan. I was baffled by the logic of the physicians. They were assuming that his pain was somehow not real, but his behavior, the most powerful evidence available, strongly indicated otherwise. More importantly, there was a potent element of doubt in all of this. They *thought* the stones might be too high to cause such pain; they *thought* the problem might be his malformed brain, even though they could not say with any certainty how that might be linked to his screams and contortions. To my mind, if there was any question, shouldn't they make the opposite assumption, that the pain might be real and that the more humane course was to treat the apparent discomfort now and work out the theoretical possibilities later?

We pressed them to medicate him. They grudgingly responded, pushing morphine and other pain-killers into his veins. But always the response came after Aidan was already screaming in distress. Maureen asked why they did not set up a morphine drip, a constant flow of the drug to keep the pain at bay altogether until more decisive treatment was possible. The doctors hesitated at this. To their minds, if this was not *real* pain, a morphine drip was useless: it would simply mask the actual neurological condition. But they had no other answers, no other suggestions for how to attack the underlying problem and make the screaming go away.

One night when I was staying with Aidan and Maureen was home resting as best she could, he began to cry. The sobs intensified until he suddenly went silent. His whole body tensed tight as he drew in as much air as his lungs would hold, his face turning deep scarlet, his fists clenched and his face stretched in exertion. Then, he exploded. His piercing scream reverberated in the large and dark four-person room, washing into every corner and returning amplified into the center. He followed that first blast with others, settling into a steady shout that rose and fell with his gasping breaths. No one else was in the room with us; his shrieks filled only my ears before they spilled out the door and down the hall.

The on-duty resident, a broad-shouldered and stocky young man, came in to see what had caused the outburst. I told him we needed morphine now. He paused, no doubt reviewing in his head the diagnosis of his superiors, but then agreed, relenting in the face of Aidan's obvious need. It would be tricky, however. In his struggle against the pain, Aidan had dislodged his IV. To get the pain-killing medicine into him quickly and effectively, another line would have to be established right away. But with his body taught in duress, Aidan presented a certain challenge. Even at the best of times his veins were thin and weak; now, with his screams and constriction, it would be very difficult to get a needle into his bloodstream.

The husky resident called in another young physician and a nurse, both men, and we set about trying to get an IV line into Aidan. It was a very masculine moment, four adult men pressing over Aidan's small, hot body. We used our strength to pin him down and hold him steady, searching for a fat vein, a way in for Sister Morphine. The talk was short and decisive.

"You hold that arm down; I'll try this vein; what size needle?"

We ignored his cries, our male defenses solid and steady. The lead doctor poked steel in his skin; once, twice, three times, to no avail; the elusive veins dodged his thrusts. I could smell sweat and nerves. Aidan's screaming continued unabated, the abdominal pain much greater than the jabs to his wrists and feet and hands. Time was suspended in darkness and heat and frustration.

Finally it was done. One of them—I forget which— struck blood at last. The small syringe was squeezed and the clear liquid ran through the thin plastic tube and into his vein and, eventually, his central nervous system. It was a large dose. The lead resident, after our prolonged wrestling match, now knew that we had to overwhelm him with the narcotic to subdue the demon in his belly.

Still, the senior doctors believed that this was not genuine pain from kidney stones, but some sort of strange neurological phantom. They moved us down the hall to a smaller two-person room where we stayed by ourselves, alone in our double aberrancy: the child with rare brain malformations and newly unnerving behavior.

Two weeks had passed since we came to Springfield and Aidan was worse than when we arrived. Maureen and I were past tolerable limits. On more than one occasion, we had pointedly yelled at doctors or nurses or whoever might be in a position to help but were failing this child. It was Maureen who finally turned the disbelieving bureaucracy to Aidan's rescue. She stormed out of the room one afternoon and stood in front of the busy nurses station, crowded with technicians and doctors and specialists, and tearfully bellowed in her loudest voice that her boy was screaming and no one was doing anything. When would somebody take this seriously and give him what he needed? In the uncomfortable silence that followed, the head nurse put her arm around her and ushered her back to the room where Aidan lay crying.

"I know what you mean," she said, "and it's going to stop now."

With that, the nurse turned and walked toward the PICU to summon the formidable chief there.

He came in with a wordless nod of the head. Standing next to the bed, he listened as the head nurse reviewed the events of the past two weeks and reported that Maureen wanted a central line to be placed, a larger intravenous port that would go directly into a major chest vein, instead of the smaller and less reliable peripheral IVs that kept failing. A central line would also facilitate a morphine drip, a constant and steady flow of medicine to prevent pain, not just respond after the pain had started. The scruffy-haired PICU chief fixed Maureen with his strong stare and raised his eyebrows, looking for her consent. She nodded silently. No words were needed; he knew what she wanted, what had to be done. He turned to the nurse and said that he would be ready in the PICU in ten minutes to place a central line.

With that, we gained better control over Aidan's pain, though at the cost of his consciousness. The unbroken stream of morphine dulled his senses; his eyes glazed over in half-aware torpor. At least he was no longer crying as hard as he was. Occasionally, when he would "break through" the narcotic effect and cry out, the morphine was supplemented with other drugs. Valium seemed to be most effective, easing him away from distress and back into sleepy stupefaction. But how much was enough?

Maureen ran into this difficult question a day or so later. She was there with him; I was at work, trying to hold the home front together as best I could. Aidan was "breaking through" regularly, falling back into torment. She asked the doctors to increase the morphine drip. They said that if they did, it would put him in danger of respiratory arrest; the palliative effect of the drug would bring perilously slow breathing. It was an impossible choice of more pain or less air. Maureen, determined to comfort her baby, opted for the latter, praying that Aidan's lungs would keep working. As she sat there, next to his bed, watching his chest rise and fall, counting as his breaths diminished from ten a minute to six to three, she knew he might be slipping away.

"I'm here with you, Aidan, it's okay. You're going to be fine, but if you have to leave, that's okay, too. I'm right here with you and I love you. We'll get through this all right, but if you have to go, I understand..."

She whispered these words close by his ear and as she spoke, he took a large breath in and let out a great sigh. His respirations worked back up to six and then ten.

Once we happen into the form of this body, we cannot forget it. And so it is that we wait out the end. Grappling and tangling with things, we rush headlong toward the end, and there's no stopping it. It's sad, isn't it? We slave our lives away and never get anywhere, work ourselves ragged and never find our way home. How could it be anything but sorrow? People can talk about never dying, but what good is that? This form we have soon becomes others, and the mind vanishes with it. How could it be called anything but great sorrow? Life is total confusion. Or is it that I'm the only one who's confused?

Of course, Chuang Tzu is not confused. He sees clearly that our lives, all lives, are contingent and limited: we happen into the form of this body and we never find all that we are looking for. Random biological processes pair a conscious mind with a physical being and then we are buffeted by the demands of society and mortality. We work to succeed, however success may be defined, but cannot escape death and, with that, we disappear back into the vast and wide Way. Even if we think we can leave a legacy of some sort, it is not really ourselves that we leave, but only material to be used and changed by those who come after. Our lives are finished when they are finished. Any expectation beyond this hard reality brings only sorrowful disappointment.

His point is not to drown us in sadness, but rather to put our busy, goal-driven lives into perspective. He is describing what he sees as the human condition—even from the distance of twenty-five hundred years, he captures the frenzy of our modern lives. So get used to it, he seems to be saying. Drop your self-importance. However accomplished we may think we are, our imagined victories are mere conceits in the face of the physical demise that awaits us all. A little less pride and a little more sympathy is warranted.

There may even be happiness here, in good Taoist fashion, on the flip-side of the sorrow. If we grasp the futility of rushing and grappling with things, then maybe we could just slow down. Do less. Do nothing, perhaps, at least for a while. And, in the end, we will find ourselves in the place we would have been anyway, whatever we tried to do. Yes, the mind will vanish; but so what? By staring that inevitability straight in the eye, we might be released; we might find our way home.

These thoughts floated through my head as I sat and watched Aidan. He was comfortably benumbed by his morphine and Valium cocktail. The pain had been subdued, vanquished by a warm unconsciousness suffused through his limp body.

Is my life better than his? Is his somehow less than mine?

Most people would quickly answer yes to both. It is just so obvious: I can walk and talk and see and write; I have felt the full range of human emotion; I am not hemmed in by mental retardation but can give full run to my mind and its thoughts; I have loved in ways he will never. How can our two lives even begin to be compared?

But Chuang Tzu would give me pause. I am also caught up in the frenetic workaday world. Although I can point to an array of achievements—a Ph.D., a good job, publications—I often wonder if I really am getting anywhere. At times I feel enslaved to the demands of economy and society: I've got to succeed in the job to earn enough to pay the mortgage, the car payments, and the raft of monthly bills; got to make enough to cover the health insurance; got to put something away for Margaret's college; got to do this, got to do that; got to propitiate the vengeful gods of consumption and production and savings and investment; got to live the modern life. So much of what I have to do is beyond my control, grappling and tangling with things...

And there Aidan lies, completely disconnected from such worries. There is so much he cannot do, but also so much he does not have to do. He does nothing, but nothing is left undone. The form of his body limits him, but so does mine. His limitations are more severe than mine, but we experience many of the same things. He hears the sound of his friends around him; he smells the sweet warmth of spring; he feels the softness of the pillow in his bed; he knows the love of his family. Our differences will not keep us from the same end. Indeed, our greatest difference may be that he will likely get there before me. Maybe he is now what I will be in a couple of more decades, when I am supine in a hospital, pumped full of drugs to chase away the pain that torments my failing organs. And after that, when my atoms are scattered on the four winds, when my dust swirls together with his and everyone else's, how different will we be then?

I can hear the voice of the brash skeptic in my ear: "if his life is no worse than yours, would you trade him?"

No, I would not. His differences really do deprive him of certain kinds of happiness, ways of being that I know how to explore and enjoy. I would not choose his way. It would be dishonest to him to pretend that his disability does not significantly circumscribe his experience. Whatever liberation there might be in his incapacity, it comes at a high cost. Yet while I would not swap lives, he has shown me the smallness of mine and the expansiveness of his.

Graham found some evidence for his conjecture about neurological decline. Early in the third week of our ordeal, he came into the room, trailed by the sullen house pediatrician, and showed me the most recent MRI images. As he held the dark film to the window to catch the light, he pointed to a row of small gray and white ovals. I looked closer and saw that they were cross-sections of the top of a skull, the folds and curls of the brain quite visible in the contrasting hues. He placed his finger on a thin, white area along the top of the brain, just inside the cranial cavity. Taking another MRI film from two years earlier, he showed me how there was less white in that picture than in the new one. This white shading was empty space, he said, a gap between the top of the brain and the skull. What was happening, he explained, was "brain atrophy." Aidan's brain was not growing at a normal rate; his head was expanding faster than his cortex, creating a breech between tissue and bone. His brain was, in effect, shrinking in proportion to his body.

Or that, at least, is what appeared to be happening. All there was to go on at this stage were two points in time, the old MRI and the new one, not quite enough to establish firmly that Aidan's brain was, indeed, atrophying. Another MRI, in a year or so, would tell for certain how much or how little Aidan's brain was growing. The attending pediatrician, her arms folded across her chest, radiated self-assurance.

When he showed me these pictures and gave his interpretation, Graham was enthusiastic and animated. His eyes shone with the excitement of a new discovery. He spoke rapidly, linking his observations to symptoms and syndromes. I could see the scientist in him celebrating fresh data, the path to a new, maybe better, explanation. I could feel the fervor. Letting myself be swept up in the moment, I welcomed the breakthrough: we were learning something new here; we were seeing pictures of how Aidan was developing over time; we were gaining a fuller understanding of his neurological profile. Science was progressing.

But just after Graham left, I realized the uselessness of this new information. It did not lead us to more effective treatment of Aidan's apparent pain. To the contrary, it encouraged the doctors in their belief that it was not *real* pain. And that left us with little to do but marvel at our extraordinarily unusual condition and bemoan our incredibly bad luck. More importantly, the kidney stones were still there and they offered a simpler—the scientists might say more parsimonious—explanation of Aidan's discomfort. Although they were supposedly too high in the kidneys to be fully potent, it was common knowledge that stones were very painful. It was much less clear how or why Aidan's brain atrophy might be the cause of his screaming. Underneath it all, Graham had provided only an observation, not a concrete causal link. Faced with the choice of a well-known source of pain or an underdeveloped neurological theory, we put our money on the kidney stones and pressed harder to have a pediatric urologist examine Aidan more closely.

Maureen had been working on just this for some time. She had negotiated the medical diplomacy of bringing another specialist into the case when the doctors thought it was unnecessary. This had led her to another hospital in Springfield, where a staff urologist with experience with children performed advanced treatment of kidney stones. She had talked with him on the phone a couple of times, but he had not yet had a chance to come and see Aidan for himself. We were waiting for him.

It was the Sunday before Thanksgiving. I was sitting next to Aidan's bed, the one closest to the door of the two-person room. Another child had been admitted into the bed next to ours, perhaps because the morphine drip had quieted Aidan down to an occasional cry. Most of the time he was unconscious or close to it. I was alone with him that day; Maureen was back at home, spending time with Margaret. The curtain was drawn between the two beds and our space was cramped. The room was quiet, the hospital slowed to a weekend pace. In the early afternoon tedium, I had snapped on the television and was indifferently watching a football game with the sound off.

In strode a tall man with broad shoulders and dark features. I guessed he was Turkish, or maybe Iranian. He looked down at Aidan and me and then quickly shifted his gaze up to the television on the wall.

"How are they doing?" he asked, a slight accent in his voice. "Are the Patriots still ahead?"

"Uh…yeah, they are." I had not been following closely but at least knew the score.

He watched one play and I could tell he was a fan. Then he turned back to me, extended his large hand and introduced himself. This was Dr. Saadi, pediatric urologist. I started to explain our situation to him, the discovery, three weeks ago, of the kidney stones, the questions about whether they were really causing pain, the alternative theory of neurological decline. Saadi was already familiar with the case. He had read the sonogram reports and various other notes and charts. As we talked, his easygoing manner put me at ease.

"Could these stones be hurting him?" I asked.

"Oh sure. You never know with kidney stones."

"Is there anything we can do to help him?"

"Yes, yes, we can break them up with a lithotripsy."

He went on to describe lithotripsy, a relatively non-invasive procedure that used concentrated sonic waves to penetrate the abdomen and shatter the stones, which then passed out of the body as fairly painless tiny particles in the urine. It was all very matter-of-fact. This was his world, after all, and treating kidney stones in young children was not strange to him at all. He said we could arrange the procedure for just after Thanksgiving; it was no problem, though Aidan would have to be transported to the neighboring hospital where he did his work. He quickly called his office to confirm the time and told me that he would inform the other doctors of the operation. With that, he shook my hand again, glanced up to see one more play, and then purposefully stepped out the door.

I was elated. It was so easy, so direct. Here was what he had wanted for three weeks: aggressive treatment of the kidney stones. And he did it so straightforwardly; no quizzical looks, no silent reproach of the irrational parents. The Near Eastern football fan had saved the day!

I read Aidan the *Tao Te Ching* during this hospital stay. It is a rather short book, made up of eighty-one brief passages, poems really. The edition I had with me was one my father had given me, one of his last gifts to me. He knew I had an interest in the Chinese classics and he must have seen a review of this recent translation. It was based upon some of the oldest known original texts, dating from second or third century B.C.E., rendered by a distinguished scholar of ancient Chinese religion and philosophy.

Reading aloud seemed a good thing to do, for both Aidan and myself. I had brought this book along because it was easy to read in a hospital—each short poem was a work unto itself—and because it was comforting to me. And reading to Aidan made a certain sense. He was lying there, knocked out by the drugs, serene and unmoving. His stillness made me think of what people said about the near-dead: their last sense to fail was their hearing. Maybe Aidan would be able to hear me. Even if he would never understand the

words, the familiar cadence of my voice might be recognizable and reassuring to him. I read the whole book to him,
twice, over the course of several days. There was much there
that spoke to him and me.

The Way floats and drifts;
It can go left or right.
It accomplishes its tasks and completes its affairs, and
     yet for this
it is not given a name.
The ten thousand things entrust their lives to it, and
     yet it does
not act as their master.
Thus it is constantly without desires.
It can be named with the things that are small.
The ten thousand things entrust their lives to it, and
     yet it does
not act as their master.
It can be named with the things that are great.

Therefore the Sage's ability to accomplish the great
Comes from his not playing the role of the great.
Therefore he is able to accomplish the great.

On Thanksgiving Day, Aidan passed a very large kidney
stone. I was with him in the morning, waiting for Maureen to arrive with Margaret so we could have some family

time together for the holiday. I checked his diaper and there it was, the size of a small pea, brownish-gray in color. Though merely a little pebble in my hand, it was enormous for a kidney stone. I called the resident doctor on duty, a young man who had come on service two weeks ago and knew our plight well, and showed him the damnable rock. His eyes widened in awe. It was the biggest stone he had seen in his short professional career. There were other implications as well. Here was incontrovertible proof that Aidan's pain had been real. It had not simply appeared out of the blue that day; it must have been working its way down through his system for days, bringing agony in its wake. The senior doctors had been wrong to emphasize neurological decline and hold back on vigorous treatment of the stones. The young physician understood this but did not say anything that might embarrass his superiors. The shake of his head and the glow of his eyes said quite enough.

The harvest feast of Thanksgiving has always been my favorite holiday. The mythology of Pilgrims and Indians was less important to me than the idea of celebrating a successful growing season, marking the turn of time away from the warmth of summer and early fall, and preparing for the winter cold. I have been the one in the family to take up the cooking duties on this day, roasting the stuffed fowl, whipping the sweet yams, baking pecan pies. This year, however, our setting would be more modest than usual: whatever we could manage in the hospital cafeteria. But the sense of the day was very much intact, whatever the circumstances. The passing of the stone signified the beginning of the end of this long, terrible episode.

As word got out about Aidan's very big kidney stone, the attitude of the medical staff changed. No one now thought us half crazy to be insisting on a lithotripsy. Even though the big stone had passed, there might be smaller pieces that still needed to be eliminated. The nurses sympathized with us; they knew that a good deal of torment could have been avoided had the doctors focused on the original diagnosis. The unlikable attending pediatrician did not come around; she stayed at the nurses station, busy with other cases.

Dr. Saadi did the lithotripsy the day after Thanksgiving. Aidan was trundled down to a waiting ambulance and driven three blocks to Mercy Hospital. I was struck by the aptness of the name. It was an unremarkable procedure. For it, Aidan was anesthetized and a device was placed against his side, a machine that blasted very focused sound waves in such a particular manner that the small and hard stone fragments were shattered into sand, which would flush from his bladder in a couple of days. The rest of his body was unaffected. All that was noticeable afterward were three small red spots on Aidan's back and a slight soreness around them. We got back to the big medical center later that afternoon, with Aidan comfortably unaware of what had transpired.

The next few days were taken up with weaning Aidan off the morphine that had coursed through his blood for two weeks. It would take some time to slowly take away the numbing elixir, to convince his body that it could live again, pain-free, without the addictive narcotic. He gradually woke up for longer and longer periods of time, opening his glassy eyes, searching for the sounds and feelings of normalcy. He did not cry. The screaming was past.

On one of the last days in the hospital after Thanksgiving, Graham, the neurologist, came in to see how we were faring. He needed to see how Aidan was responding to the change in medications and look for any outward manifestations of the brain atrophy the MRI had detected. While talking with Maureen, his lips tightened into a thin line and his eyebrows raised slightly.

"I'm sorry," he said.

He did not elaborate; he did not have to. He knew what we had been through for nearly a month; he knew that his diagnosis, while true in one sense, had taken time away from treating the immediate cause of Aidan's pain. It was in no way a malicious mistake. He had only been following his training, thinking as a neurologist, trying to do what he thought best for his patient. But it had all gone terribly wrong. His short apology did not explicitly acknowledge too much, yet it was important as it was. For all of the difficult medical situations we had found ourselves in over the years—and for the many more that lay ahead of us—only very rarely did a physician admit, even in the subtlest way, that his or her way of thinking had brought on unforeseen disaster. Maybe the fear of lawsuits was too great. In any event, Graham's words that day, while not able to turn back the clock and avoid the mishap, showed that he was able to step outside of himself, to let go of his ego and recognize things as they really were.

Then we went home.

8.

The Farther You Go, the Less You Know

I was travelling internationally less and less.

Just after the Singapore squabble but before Aidan's kidney stones, I had managed to attend a conference in Taiwan. It was quite an event. Many big-name American academics were brought over by a government-linked think-tank to talk about current events and trends in Communist mainland China. I was flattered to be in such company. In need of American friends, our Taiwan hosts made us into something of a quasi-official delegation. One of the more senior Americans had served as Ambassador to South Korea; so, he was continually introduced as "Mr. Ambassador," with the rest of us following in his train. We had an audience with the president of Taiwan and a formal dinner with the foreign minister. Some of the Foreign Ministry people had heard about my contretemps with the prime minister of Singapore, which was a minor political rival of the more democratic Taiwan, and we laughed about it. On the long flight home, across the Pacific Ocean and over the continental United States, I replayed the scenes in my head:

stern guards staring straight ahead at the president's office; smooth diplomats working the crowd; serious people debating important international topics.

But that was the last trip I would take to Asia for some years. The agony of the kidney stones reminded me of how bad things could get. I could not just fly away from Aidan's growing number of ailments.

Instead, I found myself being drawn into small-town public school politics. This had started some years earlier, when Aidan turned three and first entered pre-kindergarten. There was a group at the elementary school—the Parents Advisory Council, or PAC—that met monthly to discuss "special education" issues. I wandered into one meeting at the beginning of Aidan's first year in the school to try and learn something about how the system worked and what we might expect from it. I didn't walk away until six years later.

At that first meeting of the PAC, there was a faction of parents, mothers all, whose children had been in the school for years. They had fought many battles with the school administration to gain programs and funding for their disabled children; they had battled bravely and paved the way, with lawsuits when necessary, for those of us who came later. As a result, the kids in wheelchairs were not hidden away in separate classrooms, only to be seen at the beginning and end of each day. No, the veteran parents had demanded, and eventually won, a more inclusive atmosphere. As Aidan moved into and up through the school, he would be involved in regular classrooms. His physical therapist would come right into the room with the other kids and take him through his paces. He would sit in the reading group and listen as the other kids mastered their lessons. For all of his limitations, he would be a member of the class.

But these same parents, who had helped make the school more open and accessible for disabled kids, were set in their ways. One mother in particular was stubbornly uncompromising when it came to her own children. She would threaten and insult and malign any school employee who did not do things just the way she wanted. Her knowledge of special education law and procedure was immense and she was quite willing to call in whatever authorities she thought necessary to get her way. If she did not like a therapist or a teacher's aide or whomever, she would attack and pressure and vilify until they quit the school in disgust. The staff dreaded and avoided her. An icy chill of hostility pervaded the building when she moved through it.

Some other parents, most of them new to the school, took a different tack. They wanted to create a more positive feeling about special education. They wanted to be more cooperative with the school administration, more supportive of teachers and staff. Not wanting to alienate their children or themselves, they were looking to remake the PAC, to bring in new leadership and reach out to the larger school community.

A certain tension animated that first meeting, with two or three battle-scarred parents backing up their tenacious matron versus a smattering of newer folks sizing up the possibilities for change. We sat in a circle of small child-sized chairs in the middle of the school library, arrayed in our respective alliances. The key issue was an arcane plan to reorganize the administrative duties of the special education staff at the school. The superintendent said he wanted to shift responsibilities around to streamline operations. The veteran parents suspected that he was only trying to squeeze money out of the program by making fewer people do more work. I found myself with the newcomers, siding with the administrators. Why not trust them to do their best? Why not give something new a try? We had the numbers and carried the day. Over the opposition of the more experienced members, the PAC endorsed the Superintendent's proposal that night.

At the next meeting, I was nominated and elected chair of the PAC. This was sheer politics, since I had no experience or expertise with public school special education. More significant to the new parents, I was not from the entrenched faction. But I shared something with the more militant mothers: we were the parents of the most severely disabled children— perhaps they thought I would be able to understand their position. Whatever the case, a majority of people in the room believed I could mediate the differences in the group, and they made me chair.

I had never done anything like this before, never been drawn into community affairs. The academic life in which I had been immersed for years did not easily allow for such things. There were books to read, articles to write, theories and arguments to propound. That was what I did and I was used to the relative isolation of scholarship. But now I was being drawn into the social tumult of civic activism. I would have to figure out what the key issues were and where various people stood on them. I would have to negotiate and compromise in a realm I scarcely knew. It seemed a bit crazy. My skills in analyzing Chinese politics would be useless here—or so I thought at the outset. My senior academic colleagues would certainly look askance at this detour from the conventional professional path. Yet this was where Aidan was leading me, and I had to do it to understand his life's chances and to make them better if I could.

In our monthly meetings, we discussed various matters of special education. How could the school do better in including children with many different disabilities in regular classrooms? How could kids in wheelchairs partake of field trips to hard-to-access places? How could summer school programs be established to meet the needs of the disabled? How could we improve communications between teachers and parents and administrators? We talked and thought and pushed and pulled at the issues. Whatever the differences among us, these gradually receded as our common interest in getting what our kids needed brought us together.

I came to respect the most formidable mother. She could be obstinate and aloof, but as I got to know her I could see that her demands were often reasonable. A single parent of modest means, she had adopted several children with severe disabilities. The federal and state government encouraged precisely this kind of activity to get orphans and wards out of stultifying and dehumanizing institutions. Clearly, the care she provided for her kids was vastly superior to what they would have experienced in state-run homes and hospitals, but she needed public support to do it. Because most state services for disabled children were, by law, dispensed through public schools, she had to deal with special education administrators to get the physical therapy, speech lessons, adaptive technology, and all the things her kids required. This was a lonely battle. The school worried about money; she had to look out for her kids. Education financing was organized in such a way that programs for the disabled drew resources away from the regular curriculum. She knew how to use the law to get what she wanted, but it was easy for parents of typical children, the vast majority of the school community, to see this one woman as a selfish obstacle to the common good.

She was my ally at times. Once she suggested that we should have the superintendent address the PAC on how the school was working to include disabled children throughout all of the grade levels. This struck me as a good topic of conversation. I made the necessary arrangements and put the item on our agenda.

It was March, before the midwinter vacation, in the midst of a long stretch of school days that wore on everyone. By this time, I had been the PAC chair for over a year; Aidan was now four and a half years old. That evening, the usual group of about twelve parents sat on the small chairs in the library. A stuffed owl peered down at us menacingly from its perch on the wall. We were joined this night by the superintendent, a tall man with sandy hair and a tie; he held a manila folder of notes. He had asked one of the special education teachers to come and make a presentation on an innovative new team-teaching system they had developed. She had long frizzy hair and wire-rim glasses, the look of a hippie, if it had been twenty-five years earlier. No refreshments were served.

I called the gathering to order. We approved the minutes of the last meeting and then turned our attention to the superintendent and the teacher. He began with a description of how two sixth-grade teachers had combined their classes and, with the help of the special education teacher, devised new ways to address the broad range of needs of all of their students. The kids with learning disabilities were given extra attention, as were the most advanced learners. There was one child with more severe physical limitations, but he had his own aide who took charge of his program. The superintendent's eyes shone as he told us all this; he was obviously quite happy and believed that this arrangement was effective and efficient. Next to him, the special education teacher chimed in with a few more details and several assurances that everything was "great!"

The minatory mother was ready with her reply. Why, she asked, was all the time of one special education teacher being expended on only two classes, a total of about forty-five children? This left only three other special education teachers to cover all the rest of the school, some twenty-six other classes, more than five hundred students. And what was happening in the lower grades, where, it appeared to her, insufficient staff was available?

The superintendent stared blankly for a moment, perhaps turning over in his mind all the trouble this mother has caused him in recent years, and then repeated how wonderfully the sixth grade program was working.

The mother sneered dismissively and looked sideways at one of her comrades, raising her eyebrows in knowing disgust.

Another parent spoke up, questioning the wisdom of using so much scarce special education staff time in the sixth grade. Wouldn't it make better sense to spend more time in the earlier grades in the hopes of catching and correcting some of the learning disabilities so that they might be solved by the sixth grade?

Seemingly determined to avoid public discussion of the weaknesses of special education, the superintendent, a defensive tone seeping into his voice, talked about how various aides were working closely with teachers in the early grades to handle the children with special needs, and everyone was working hard to do a good job, and how staff was short all over, and money was short and....He was speaking faster and louder.

The meeting descended from that point to a near shouting match, mostly between the superintendent and the main mother, but with others weighing in: attacking, defending, trying to settle things down. I had lost control of the floor and, finally, had to adjourn the meeting in a billow of bad feelings all around.

This was not Chinese politics; it was not the prime minister of Singapore or the president of Taiwan. But it was surely politics, a combustible admixture of conflicting interests and incompatible personalities. The eruption of the meeting had saddened me. I knew all the players and could see that each had good intentions. Yet circumstances—some beyond our control, others of our own making—conspired against us that night. Maybe that's how politics works, maybe the dynamics of the moment, the rush of emotions in an uncomfortable setting, can harden into unforgiving words and indelible impressions. Maybe Chairman Mao had known something of this.

No need to leave your door to know the whole world;
No need to peer through your windows to know the Way
*   of Heaven.*
The farther you go, the less you know.

Therefore the Sage knows without going,
Names without seeing,
And completes without doing a thing.

—*Tao Te Ching, section 33, Hendricks*

(47)

I do not wholly accept Lao Tzu's point here.

Before I had gone to China for the first time, I had studied ten semesters of the language over four years; I had taken a wide variety of classes on Chinese politics, history, and economics; I had read countless books and articles and begun research on my own dissertation. But it was only when I went there that I really felt like I started to know something about it. Strolling through the back gardens of the Summer Palace in Beijing, admiring the gracious architecture, watching families picnic by the side of the lake, I realized that I had to unlearn much of what I thought I knew about China from my studies in the U.S. My previous knowledge was not wholly invalid, but it had to be reconfigured in the face of direct observation of Chinese realities. The farther I had gone, the more I knew.

Of course, in another way, at another level, Lao Tzu is right. If what we want to know about is broader than any particular place, if we want to see how myriad specific things fit together into an organic whole—*know the whole world*—then travel is unnecessary. The "Heaven" he refers to is not a transcendent space of eternal redemption in the Christian sense; rather, it is the destiny born of natural processes. It is not a predetermined endpoint toward which everything moves, but an ever-unfolding fate beyond the ken of human comprehension. It is something more than mankind, but something less than Way (*Tao*), of which it is a part. And if we want to know the Way of Heaven, we do not even need to leave our home.

How can we know everything in the world and, beyond that, the Way of Heaven, without seeing or doing a thing? Because Way, the totality of Heaven and Earth, can be found everywhere and extends to all things individually and together. What appears to be the most parochial experience, then, reveals as much of Way as the most cosmopolitan life. If we find Way in our own lives, we need not look further.

There is a radical universalism here, but not a denial of difference. It matters not whether we are speaking of Chinese or Americans, men or women, the disabled or the abled. Whatever the category, each, in its own way, is an expression and an element of Way. What I see in China is just what I see in PAC meetings in my small-town school library, which is the same as what I see when I stand, at night, silently by Aidan's bedside: a dense variety of shapes and forms and lives and lots, sometimes clashing, sometimes meshing, but always being and becoming together.

We lived in the shadow of that terrible *status epilepticus*, the one that had set Aidan back so badly when he was only two. Through all that had happened for about four years, his entering school, his kidney stones, it did not recur, but we were never quite sure if it would. The seizures came daily but did not crescendo into that unstoppable neurological havoc. Yet it could happen again. The medications were always imperfect; the doctors were never certain. Any one seizure could be the beginning of another big one. It was a constant threat gnawing at whatever serenity we might find.

At the start of the new year following the Thanksgiving of the kidney stones, it did happen again. Aidan was six. He was growing steadily in size, though his physical and mental capacities had changed hardly at all since he was an infant. He still did not stand or walk or see or talk. We had kept him in the preschool class, which suited him developmentally. He looked older than his schoolmates, his features longer and sharper than the plump three- and four-year-olds around him. He looked older but could never match their abilities. But we were not thinking of the contrast with his classmates that winter. It was the holidays, the day after New Year's, a fresh start, a happy time.

On an evening like most others, after dinner, about six o'clock, Aidan was in his bed. He often got tired and cranky at the end of the day and found some comfort in his blankets and pillows. There he was when Maureen noticed a new kind of seizure that we had first seen a few days before. His left arm contracted, fisted hand rising slowly to shoulder; his left knee lifted slightly off the mattress. He went into a slow-motion myoclonic jerk but just on the left side of his body. After about fifteen seconds, this changed into a generalized tonic-clonic episode, which, in ten more seconds, evolved into a laughing seizure, his body stretched and rigid. A week earlier, he came out of this new pattern after about a minute or so, without any immediate recurrence. On the second day of January, however, he kept doing it.

One sequence—slow contraction, rapid tonic-clonic, elongated laughter—was followed, in about two or three minutes, by another. And then another. After the fifth repetition, Maureen and I quickly decided that we needed to give him some of the medications we kept on hand for more ominous seizures. With her nurse's skill, Maureen drew up into a small syringe four milligrams of a special intravenous Valium solution. She then twisted off the needle and administered this dose into his rectum, like a suppository. Dr. Graham had recommended this procedure for emergencies. The drug would, in this manner, absorb into his bloodstream more quickly than it would from his stomach. And we did not have to worry about finding a vein for a direct injection. Four milligrams of Valium was a stout dose for a six-year-old. We waited for his unconsciousness.

After about twenty minutes, nothing had changed. He was still in it, the same strange convulsion repeating over and over, the high pitch of his screechy laugh echoing off the walls. We gave him four more milligrams of Valium and called the doctor.

Graham was not on duty. One of his partners, a calm and polite man who we had met in the hospital after the first *status epilepticus*, called back. Maureen crisply reported what was happening. The doctor knew us; he knew Maureen was a nurse; he knew that we had just spent a terrible November in the hospital and that we would prefer not to go to the local Emergency Room if we could help it. He gave Maureen instructions and told her to call him back if things did not get better.

We waited fifteen more minutes and, with the seizures still firing, hit him with four more milligrams of Valium as the doctor had ordered. This brought the total up to twelve milligrams in about an hour, a considerable load for a little boy.

The laughing seizures only seemed to last a little longer, twisting his mouth into a unnerving smile, raising his eyebrows in faux joy. After twenty more minutes of the cruel chortle, we gave him yet another four milligrams.

Finally, it stopped. About an hour and a half had passed. Our concentration had been fixed on getting over this, our senses heightened by the hazard. I was not scared, however; not like last time. If the definition of *status epilepticus* is a prolonged seizure lasting longer than fifteen minutes, then this had certainly been one. But it did not seem as dangerous. Death did not feel near. Perhaps it was the on-and-off nature of the attack, one minute of seizure, two minutes rest, one minute of seizure, two minutes of rest, over and over. Maybe the pauses somehow broke the tension and kept our anxiety from escalating quite so far. Or maybe it was that we were home in familiar and unthreatening surroundings. Or that we were just inured to deadly possibilities. Whatever the reason, I had not been frightened; and it was gone now in any case.

We put Margaret down in her bed next to Aidan's. Though almost four at the time and generally aware that her brother was not like most other children, she was oblivious to the fact that something bad had just happened. Maureen and I had been able to remain calm enough through it all to ward off any immediate sense of danger for her. Margaret settled down easily, and shortly thereafter, with stress-induced fatigue creeping in upon us, we went to bed as well. Sleep emptied my mind. Unremembered dreams danced in my head. Darkness. Silence. Stillness....

My eyes bolted open suddenly as Aidan's piercing laugh shattered my slumber. Time slowed, seconds seemed like minutes, as I came to realize what the sound meant. Maureen was up before me. I followed her into the children's room and looked down at Aidan, just as he started into the slow motion left-side myoclonic contraction.... It had come back. It was about two o'clock in the morning and the heavy dose of Valium in his bloodstream had evidently thinned enough to allow the electrical storm to start up again.

We called the doctor. It was Graham's partner again and he was, as usual, even-tempered. Knowing we still had an even stronger anticonvulsant on hand, he did not order us to the hospital. Instead we were to give Aidan five milligrams of intravenous Versed solution per rectum.

Versed is similar to Valium—they are both in the benzodiazepine family of drugs—only stronger. By some reckonings, it is three to four times more powerful than Valium. The *Physician's Desk Reference*, a standard pharmacological source for descriptions of drugs, reports the following:

> Intravenous Versed has been associated with respiratory depression and respiratory arrest.... In some cases...death or hypoxic encepholapathy has resulted.... The initial intravenous dose for conscious sedation may be as little as

1 mg, but should not exceed 2.5 mg in a normal healthy
adult...

Of course, we were not giving this to Aidan directly into
his vein; so, the effect would not be quite as powerful. And
we were not attempting to keep him conscious and sedate.
Yet even though five milligrams was, no doubt, the proper
dose for what we faced, it was a big and potentially dangerous assault on Aidan's central nervous system, especially
with the leftover Valium still lingering in his body. It was
enough to knock me, a 185-pound adult male, unconscious.

We waited. Five minutes became ten became fifteen.
The eerie laughing still came at the end of the same series of
seizures. The Versed was not stopping it. The awesome
power of the *status* was more than even this very potent drug
could control. The monster was not yet slain.

One more option was available to us before a retreat to the
hospital would be necessary. The doctor had calculated, given
Aidan's size and the severity of the seizures, that his little body
could tolerate one more double-dose of Valium. Maureen was
still steady enough to draw up the eight milligrams and give
it to him. It was hard to fathom. Over the course of the entire
crisis, Aidan now had absorbed twenty-four milligrams of
Valium and five milligrams of Versed. A perilous limit had
been reached. We had an oxygen tank in the closet, left over
from our struggles with pneumonia, and I made a mental
note of it as the crushing weight of the drugs pressed down on
Aidan's lungs.

Maureen and I stood and watched. She was quietly counting his breaths per minute. His left hand came up to his shoulder, but more slowly than ten minutes ago. He went into the tonic-clonic shaking, but not quite as intensely. His laugh was a bit quieter. Gradually, the seizures melted away: each motion shorter and lazier than the time before, each sound more subdued. Soon his body was just gently shaking a little and then, finally, slumped motionless into a deep, unwakable sleep.

It had not been anything like the first *status*. The harsh lights of the hospital and the frightening newness of it all had, that first time, made us fear for his life. This time we had a better sense of what we were up against. I was strangely free from worry. Would the seizures come back yet again? Would they take a developmental toll on him? Would he ever wake up? I did not dwell on these sorts of thoughts; they did not force themselves on me. As I lay there, back in bed, staring into the deepening darkness, I marveled more than anything else: at the mysterious power of the seizures; at Aidan's resilience against them; and at the extraordinary little victory we had just won in our own home.

In yielding is completion.
In bent is straight
In hollow is full.
In exhaustion is renewal.
In little is contentment.

In much is confusion.

—*Tao Te Ching, section 22*

Aidan presses his feet down hard against the frame of his wheelchair. He pushes his back into the seat, extending his hips forward and pulling the safety belt tight to his waist. His head moves back and to the left. With every muscle taught, he fights against the cold confines of the chair. He wants to stretch, to move, to rise up and transcend the bounds of his body. But he cannot do it alone, cannot lift himself up and away, break free and run and jump and explode in little-boy energy.

Since he turned six or so, we reach this point every day, perhaps several times every day. He needs to change position. Depending on the circumstances, we might lay him in his bed on his belly, which allows him to draw himself up, arching his back high, almost straight up, and raising his head defiantly. He defeats gravity for a few moments. The muscles in his upper back and neck are remarkably strong from these exercises. He hardly uses his arms at all to push up; he relies on the steely sinews that run along his spine. He is powerful in his way.

When I am with him at these times, and not distracted by other duties, I will take him in my lap. Sliding my right arm behind his shoulders and slipping my left under his buttocks, I lift him from his bed or chair, folding him inwards at his waist. He is not a toddler anymore and I can feel my biceps tighten against his weight. I curl him snug to my chest and sit down on the couch. He fights back. It is our version of rough-housing: he thrusting back to straighten himself as best he can, and I bending him back to sit on my lap. I am still stronger than he, still the alpha-dog of our pack, and after a minute or two of loving struggle, he is nestled there under my chin.

We sit like this for at least a half an hour at a time, sometimes a full hour, almost every day. When he was smaller, I could manage to hold a book while supporting him, and I would read aloud to him, and Margaret if she joined us. He's bigger and stronger now and reading is not possible in quite the same way it used to be. So we just sit there. After a time he relaxes in my arms. Often I will watch the television news, just to keep connected to the world at large. I keep the sound low, however, so that, for him, it melts into the background clatter of the household. My breathing is steady and slow; this is what he feels, the gentle rhythm of my chest rising and falling, lulling him to sleep. And his restfulness runs back into me; my shoulders let loose, releasing the tensions there and deeper inside. He naps peacefully, the warmth of our two bodies mixing and mingling between us.

We do this most days, sit together, transported for a time from the to and fro of our lives, calmed on the couch, the two of us. And from there we can *know the whole world.*

The road to Boston was familiar. For this trip, we would get on the Massachusetts Turnpike and drive straight across the state. It would take us about three hours driving time to get to the center of the city. I knew the way; we had done this drive before. Once, just for fun, we took both kids and spent a summer weekend doing family things: the Children's Museum, the Science Museum, the "Make Way for Ducklings" statue at the Boston Public Gardens. All of these places were fairly wheelchair friendly and agreeable for both Aidan and Margaret. Another time, we had driven in for a consultation with the Neurology Department at Children's Hospital Boston, which is where we were headed this fine March day.

It had been a couple of years since we were last at Children's Hospital but I still had a clear memory of how to get there and where to park. It was a sprawling yet compact facility. The entrance was set back off of Longwood Avenue, the epicenter of Boston's renowned medical community. The driveway curled in and under the central section of the complex, sheltered beneath overhanging floors above. Parking attendants went about their business, ticketing the cars and moving them out to neighboring lots. We unloaded Aidan's wheelchair from the back of the station wagon, lifted him into it, and the four of us swept through the extralarge revolving door and into the lobby.

Two large fish tanks just to the right of the main entryway caught Margaret's eye immediately. It was her first time here. She was captivated by the colorful fish and the bustling people and the newness of it all. A little further back in the lobby was a kinetic sculpture, a miniature roller-coaster–like track on which small colored wooden balls, about one inch in diameter, rolled and dipped. At some points, small conveyor belts would lift the balls, one at a time, spaced about ten seconds apart, up to a higher section of the track about six feet above the floor. They would then twist and turn their way down and around, sometimes running smoothly, sometimes clinking down small xylophone stairs, sometimes shooting out into the air and landing precisely on the next part of the track to continue on incessantly. The motion and the noise drew the children's attention. Margaret stood and gazed in wonderment. I did as well. The crazy routine of the balls, moving over and over again through a dizzying maze, up and down and around, was something every parent of a disabled child knew.

Our purpose was a twenty-four-hour EEG. Aidan would be admitted overnight, perhaps for two nights, depending on how things went. Twenty-four electrodes would be pasted on his head, the wires bundled together in back and connected to unseen computers that would record and analyze every electrical impulse in his head. He would be plugged in for a full day to give the doctors a broader view of his brain activity. Being leashed to the machine would not be too much of a burden for him. We could sit him up in his wheelchair, though he had to be kept close by the bed to stay within reach of the wires. He could not be pushed about or go outside, but it was just for a day or two and, soon enough, we would be on our way home to all of his usual sensations and smells and sounds.

The data gathered from the EEG would provide a baseline of information, against which we could measure the effectiveness of the newest antiseizure technology we were planning to use: a vagus nerve stimulator, VNS. This was a small device, about the size of a heart pacemaker, implanted in the left chest of a person suffering from intractable seizures. It generated a small, intermittent electrical impulse that would run up a thin wire connected to the vagus nerve in the neck. The current generated would continue up the nerve fiber all the way into the brain. There, the theory went, it would disrupt the electrochemistry of a seizure, rather like fighting electric fire with electric fire. It was the latest innovation in seizure control, approved by the FDA less than a year before. When the doctors explained it to us, it sounded dangerous—zapping the brain—but everyone said it was safe and thoroughly tested and effective. Since all else had failed us, and the seizures could sometimes grow to truly treacherous proportions, we had to try it.

The work would be done by the neurosurgery department. I was fascinated by this group. They operated on the brains and central nervous systems of children, perhaps the most delicate work to be done in all of medicine. Implanting a vagus nerve stimulator was, for these folks, a relatively simple matter. It was not brain surgery, literally. All they had to do was make an incision in the chest to insert the VNS and another incision in the neck to connect the wire to the nerve, and that was that. It was unlikely that anything would go wrong with such a straightforward procedure, especially since these people were at the very top of their profession. This was Children's Hospital Boston, arguably the best pediatric health center in the country, maybe the world. The doctors here were affiliated with Harvard Medical School. They knew their science, their clinical practice, their professional standards. They were the best.

We had come to a mutual and unstated understanding with Graham. For all the good work he had done for us over the years, as well as the painful experience with the kidney stones, we needed a fresh pair of eyes on Aidan's brain. We needed new doctors and new treatments. Graham was good, but Children's was better and that was what we needed now. There had been no formal parting of the ways with Graham. He knew that Children's was doing the VNS. He referred us. We went and gradually shifted all of our attention there, to Boston, a longer ride away. The doctors sent him copies of all of their reports, but we would not see him again for three years.

The twenty-four-hour EEG, prelude to the VNS, was our first full introduction to Children's. Before that, we had driven in for an office visit or two. Now we were up on a floor, the neuro floor, watching as the nurses hastened about. Maureen knew what good nursing was all about and did not tolerate bad care for Aidan. If a nurse's technique was bad, or her medical knowledge inaccurate, or her manner cool, Maureen's faith in her—they were almost always women— would quickly falter and have to be earned back. She had never forgotten the older nurse in our small-town hospital who had botched Aidan's care. This would not happen at Children's. Most of the nurses on our floor had been doing pediatric neurology for years; the rest were bright newcomers, quick to learn the ins and outs of this domain of children's brains.

Setting up the EEG went smoothly. A briskly efficient nurse took Aidan's medical history and then helped the technician attach the electrodes to his head. A microphone hung from the ceiling and a video camera was trained on him from the wall. These would allow the doctors to correlate anomalous brain activity to physical sights and sounds. None of the recording machines themselves were in the room with us; they were sequestered away, down the hall, where doctors could huddle and interpret when they had to. The room showed little sign of intense medical observation. It was a quiet single, tucked into the corner of the building, with oddly angled walls. The nurse had clear answers for all our questions.

Maureen, unsurprisingly, insisted that she be the one to spend the night there with Aidan. I knew better than to try and fight that battle; so, after an hour or so, I took Margaret and set off for a nearby motel where we had reserved a room. We were trying to make this trip as fun and diverting for Margaret as possible. She had been in hospitals with us before, had wandered with me through the pediatric wing in Springfield, but as she was getting older, we did not want her to attach negative meanings to medical settings. She would, no doubt, be with us and her brother in many more places like this. I took her to the motel—always a fun thing for a four-year-old—and she delighted in the prospect of swimming in the pool with her mother later in the day. Then, with a good amount of the afternoon stretching out before us, we set off into Boston to have fun. At the Children's Museum, she lost herself in a swirl of exhibits and activities, shopping at a play grocery store, kneeling on a tatami mat in a Japanese-style house, a world away from Children's Hospital.

Maureen and Margaret did indeed swim in the motel pool that evening. I stayed in the hospital room with Aidan, dining on a sandwich from the café downstairs. Evening settled into the space, the ambiguity of dusk suffusing all. Aidan was comfortable in his bed. The hospital, although new to me, did not seem strange at all. When Maureen returned to spend the night, I left for the motel without foreboding.

Later the next morning, the doctors started coming around. There were several. They had started analyzing the data, pinpointing where in Aidan's brain the seizures started and where they went. Some of what appeared to be seizures were, they said, merely "movement disorders," something like a twitch emanating not from the brain but from elsewhere in the nervous system. There were, however, a dozen or so true seizures that they could document. They could describe these events, but they could not tell us, definitively, why they happened as they did.

The most impressive doctor of the lot was the senior pediatric neurologist. He looked to be about sixty, a shock of gray-white hair atop his medium build. Well-known for his research in the field, he spoke hardly at all. He did not have to as he was constantly surrounded by two or three younger acolytes, who were quite willing to state their opinions and wait, eyes wide, for the master's response. Maureen asked the gray-white sage his judgment of Graham's "brain atrophy" reading of Aidan's last MRI. He replied that it was probably not a matter of continuing deterioration, as the word "atrophy" implied, but, rather, a more limited effect of a discrete action, most likely that terrible sustained *status epileticus* four years earlier in our hometown hospital. The senior doctor explained this with such quiet authority—he did not raise his voice above a loud whisper—it seemed none would dare contradict him.

After the chief neurologist and his retinue proceeded out of the room, another doctor came in and introduced himself. It was a foreign name of indistinct nationality that I did not hear clearly. He spoke with a slight accent, vaguely Eastern European. His short dark hair framed black horn-rimmed glasses and a round face. He did not wear a creased white coat like his senior colleague, but, instead, donned what looked like a sports jacket with an odd brown and black pattern. Voluble and smiling, he shook my hand and reassured me that everything was going just fine.

"Things are good, you know." He held my hand and looked straight into my eyes. "The VNS, it's worked well for several people now. You will get one, too, right? Yes. And it will be good for you, too."

He nodded his head while he talked. I couldn't help smiling at him, with him.

When he left, Maureen and I turned to one another and laughed. We both had the same image in our minds: that was one "wild and crazy guy" working in the world's leading pediatric neurology unit.

I found out later that the funny doctor was Kurdish; he had come to the U.S. from either Turkey or Iraq, escaping ethnic persecution. He had no doubt seen some hard things along the way and worked diligently to get where he was. Maybe his humor was his armor, his shield for fending off the sadness of his personal past and the sorrow of his medical present, surrounded as he was by children with serious neurological problems. And it turned out that he was right: everything did go fairly well.

We returned to Children's three months later, as summer spread its June warmth, to have the VNS implanted in Aidan's chest. Our routine was similar to the time before: we all came and rented a motel room. I distracted Margaret with excursions in the city when Aidan was safely out of the operating room. Maureen was able to break the tension of the hospital and get some real sleep, while I stayed one night next to him. We recognized some of the doctors and nurses on the floor. The cheerful Kurd came by with comforting winks and nods. It was all rather familiar. The only ominous moment came when we met with the neurosurgeon before the operation. He was confident and direct, as all surgeons are. He had to tell us all the possible risks, even as he indicated that none were really likely to happen. The vagus nerve, he told us, runs right next to the carotid artery, the main conduit of blood from heart to brain. Were that bloodline to be nicked—he used the passive voice—it could cause complications. As he said this I imagined what those complications might be: major blood loss, denial of oxygen to the brain, and so on. It was just one more of those terrible possibilities that I had learned to put out of my mind; to ponder it might paralyze me with fear. Nothing so terrible came to pass. The surgeon found his way between nerve and artery, the device was positioned, the procedure successful.

Success was, as usual, only relative. The operation was completed without incident; we stayed in the hospital for observation for one night and then all returned home again. But the seizures still came. As weeks drifted into months, we sensed that the VNS might have been reducing the duration of some of his episodes. He seemed to come out of the worst of them more quickly than before. We did not rigorously record each and every seizure as some people do. Seven years of bitter medicines and dashed hopes had sapped our will to observe brain functions quite so closely. We could tell, however, that a slight improvement had been gained: not the dramatic breakthrough to seizure-free life reported by some VNS users, but, rather, a mild smoothing of the roughest convulsive edges.

We had gone to Boston, to Children's Hospital, and been impressed with their skill and care, but the rhythms of our days changed little afterward.

Joy and anger, sorrow and delight, hope and regret, doubt and ardor, diffidence and abandon, candor and reserve: it's all music rising out of emptiness, mushrooms appearing out of mist. Day and night come and go, but who knows where it all begins? It is! It just is! If you understand this day in and day out, you inhabit the very source of it all.
—*Chuang Tzu*

We try and we fail. We try again. We have to: it is our son, his health, his life. The seizures are hateful. They take him, transport him away from his own consciousness, shake his body, hurl his arms and legs, twist his face, rattle his eyes. We have to try and stop them. But we can't, not completely. It's discouraging.

The anger still comes sometimes, often set off by something simple but driven by the terrible enormity of it all. I don't throw things or break things now, but I can feel the burning on the back of my neck, the pressure in my face, the ire rising from within. If I walk away, just out of the room or outside, after a few minutes it passes. I am not bottling it up inside; it is just more transitory than it was before. Time and so many hard necessities have worn the anger down, sapped it of its strength.

And maybe I have internalized, to some degree, the realization that the bad comes with the good, the good with the bad. What seems frustrating and impossible at one moment is just *music rising out of emptiness, mushrooms appearing out of mist*. It is transitory and it will change. Indeed, to label anything as "frustrating" or "impossible" is to invest it with meanings that may well be superfluous. Listen to Chuang Tzu: *It is! It just is!* Interpreting it, whatever it may be, forces us away from this simple recognition. *It just is.*

It was a crowded kindergarten classroom, crammed full of books and supplies and creative junk of all sorts. Makeshift shelves split the room into half a dozen work areas where small groups of young students could pursue their common projects. Two doves, a hamster, and some fish made their homes in one alcove, ready to introduce biology. The requisite computer was squeezed into another corner. It seemed a fun and lively place. But narrow aisles left little room for Aidan's wheelchair and Maureen and I worried that Aidan might not fit.

Aidan was seven, two years older than the others in the class. He still could not walk or talk or see. His abilities were closer to those of a three-month-old infant. How could he possibly fit, physically and cognitively, into a kindergarten class?

Our worries were eased, though, when we saw that Leland was there. Last year, Leland had been in Aidan's preschool class just across the hall and was one of Aidan's best pals. He was always first to volunteer to push Aidan's chair, or to sit next to him at story time. Outside on the playground, Leland would find stones or plants to rub across his friend's palms. When the time had come to move up to kindergarten, Leland specifically requested to be in Aidan's room, to be near his buddy.

But that was preschool, where more attention was paid to socialization and group activities and cooperation. This was kindergarten, where the other children had to advance in their studies. They would begin to read and write, things that Aidan could never do. And as they grew intellectually, the social distance between them and Aidan would grow as well. They would notice what he was not doing, what he could not do. Perhaps they would start to see him in a different light, classify him. I had seen it in the older students, the fifth and sixth graders. In the morning, as they ambled past the door where the van dropped off the kids in wheelchairs, they commented, sometimes harshly, about the "handicaps." They were not bad kids, just unaware of the hurtful power of their words. This was what we feared about kindergarten: the beginning of the end of our boy's innocence, his introduction into a demanding and fast-paced world that would only seldom slow to appreciate him.

It did not take long to allay our fears. In a few days, the cluttered classroom was rearranged to make room for the wheelchair. Aidan was included in most facets of the class. When the other children were reading aloud, he was nearby, listening in. At craft time Cathy, his teacher's aide, made sure that his hands, too, were doused in finger paint or smeared with glue. Although he had to lie down on the couch at times when he was uncomfortable, taking him away from planned activities, the other children did not see this as odd or disruptive. They did not find it strange when his physical therapist, Kate, came into the room, laid him down on a mat, and stretched his arms and legs. If they were close, and not busy with other tasks, they would join in, happily helping to hold his foot at the proper angle or lying alongside him, whispering in his ear. Gradually, one by one, they took an interest in him, and that grew into understanding, which blossomed into affection.

School was not perfect, of course. It was still an institution ill-suited to carry out its state-mandated mission of providing services for disabled children, services that sometimes ranged beyond strictly educational matters, merging into the medical realm. Administrators had trouble finding the money, teachers had trouble adapting their curricula. But, whatever its failings, school surrounded Aidan with his peers, and they made all the difference for him by making the most of his differences.

During the second full week of school, Aidan's class was in the gym to play dodge ball. They chose up sides, and Nicholas, one of the captains, picked Aidan for his team. Then, without any prompting from anyone else, he stopped the selection. Turning to his classmates, he called out: "Okay, everybody, let's do three cheers for Aidan." And they did.

Each child added a voice to the cheerful chorus of "hip-hip-hoorays" that echoed through the cavernous room; and each flourish affirmed Aidan's place in the class.

The children understood his obvious disabilities, but they also found his unique and positive attributes. When asked why Aidan was his friend, Nicholas said, "I think Aidan is really nice. He always listens to me and that makes me feel good." It hardly mattered to him that Aidan was blind, immobile, and speechless. Nicholas had probably never heard the words "brain abnormality," "seizure disorder," or "mental retardation," and would not need such terms to describe his new pal.

Robert, another classmate, also found something special in Aidan: "I like Aidan because he has his own language. He is the only one that knows his language." Perhaps he was referring to the sounds Aidan made: the gentle coos when he was content or the mournful cries when he was upset. But language is more than mere sound and, maybe Robert also sensed how Aidan perceived and responded to his environment. If he was comfortable and surrounded by the swirling chatter of a class full of children, his wide-open unseeing eyes would brighten as he listened to the happy noise. A bad smell or taste would make him pucker his lips and shake his head in a clear sign of rejection. These, too, were parts of Aidan's language. And though he modestly said that only Aidan knew this personal dialect, Robert was obviously attuned to it as well.

After a month or so, the children were so friendly with Aidan they were no longer repelled by the disconcerting things that could happen. Seizures, to the uninitiated, were frightening. Aidan's still came in several forms: a momentary staring off into space; a series of single lightning-quick convulsions of arms and legs; a general stiffening of the entire body. The odd laughing seizure would still occur from time to time.

One day, Aidan lapsed into a laughing seizure, which could last for as long as a minute. His teacher's aide quickly stretched him out on the couch, freeing his body from the confines of the wheelchair, and kept a close eye on him. These could be tense moments, watching and waiting for the episode to pass. It was then that Monika, a girl of remarkable poise for her five years, came over to Aidan. She had been born in Bosnia and had fled, two years earlier, with her parents and little brother away from the violence of Sarajevo. Without the slightest hint of apprehension, she calmly sat down next to him and took his hand. She stayed with him until the spell had passed, until he was settled again. Monika did not ask questions of him or explain her reaction, she simply understood that Aidan was uncomfortable and needed a friend's comfort.

Such moments stood in stark contrast to the isolation that might have befallen Aidan had he been born in a different place or a different time. I was confronted with such gloomy possibilities when we drove down to my mother's house. The trip would take us past an old run-down state mental hospital. It was a sprawling campus of forlorn red brick dormitories, rusted brown bars on windows, and colorless paint flaking into oblivion. The institution was not used much these days, only a few people trod the weed-choked pathways, but it stood as a melancholy monument to the time when disabled people were shut away from society.

But that was not Aidan's life. Instead, he had his place in a chaotic kindergarten class, where he could feel a hamster scamper on his lap, hear the clamor of two dozen children, sense his friends around him. His wheelchair sometimes collided with a bookshelf and he occasionally missed out on certain activities, but he was a full-fledged member of the class. He fit.

9.

Mastering Uselessness

There is a man, an influential contemporary philosopher, who says that Maureen and I should have had the right to kill Aidan when he was an infant. Indeed, he suggests that it would have been a good thing if we had killed him.

Peter Singer teaches ethics at Princeton. He has authored or edited about thirty books and many dozens of scholarly and popular articles. His most recent collection is called *Writings on an Ethical Life*. Perhaps most famous for his defense of animal rights and vegetarianism, he has made many different kinds of arguments: that equality is morally essential; that racism and sexism are wrong; that the rich have an obligation to help the poor; and that "the killing of a defective infant is not morally equivalent to killing a person. Very often it is not wrong at all."

I can't remember when I first encountered Singer's defense of infanticide. It may have been when he burst onto the American scene with his appointment to a distinguished position at Princeton in 1999. Protests by disability rights groups ensued. He was profiled in prominent magazines and newspapers. I quite clearly recollect Maureen's fury as she learned what this man said about children like Aidan. But I was less angered than fascinated. How could he possibly say such things? Did he have some sort of extraordinary insight into the human condition that I was missing? I read his central arguments.

Singer is a utilitarian, which means he does not recognize any sort of inherent sanctity of human life. For him the value of an individual is neither granted by divine authority nor rooted in the physical fact of existence. Rather, human worth is determined by the balance of pleasure and pain a person is likely to experience over the course of his time on earth. The more happiness one adds to the total amount of human pleasure in the world, the more valuable the life; the more pain, the less valuable. For a person to fully appreciate and anticipate the many pleasures and pains of life, a certain self-consciousness and rationality are required. These, then, are central to Singer's definition of personhood. Only individuals who are self-aware and rational can understand their own interests and desires for the future. To kill such people would be bad, because they would be acutely aware of the suffering and loss of death, adding to the pain of the world.

A much looser standard applies to beings that are not wholly self-aware and rational. For such individuals— Singer does not recognize them as human persons—we can estimate for them the probable balance of pleasures and pains in their lives, since they cannot perceive these for themselves. If close family members can determine that this individual's life is miserable and will continue to be miserable, then it is morally justified, for Singer, to kill him.

Newborn infants, mentally retarded adults, and many other disabled or diseased humans are candidates for death by Singer's way of thinking. They do not even count as persons. Alternatively, many animal species, especially higher mammals who seem to exhibit characteristics of self-consciousness and, however limited, rationality, have a greater claim to personhood and life than immature or disabled humans. For Singer, it is wrong to kill an adult pig, but right to kill a disabled human infant.

However gruesome these arguments, Singer presents them with clear and seductive logic. It all starts with what appears to be a most reasonable assumption that like things must be treated alike when making ethical judgments. When he asserts that self-consciousness is central to human experience, a casual reader might nod in agreement. He moves so smoothly from point to point; he seems so smart and judicious. And then, almost before you realize it, he has justified killing Aidan.

I am not a casual reader of Singer's work. I am trained to analyze, to tear up arguments, to turn over theories; that is my day job. I knew before I had started reading where he was going. The infanticide proposition was familiar to me. What's more, I have a very personal interest in denying his conclusion that I should have killed Aidan. As I move through the text, I spot chinks in his armor: questionable assumptions, flimsy facts. The cold precision of his intellect, seemingly impervious to emotional attachments, has its weaknesses. There are various ways to come back at him, some fairly famous scholarly refutations of utilitarianism; it so easily sacrifices the interests, even the lives, of the few, for the happiness of the many. I am not a philosopher, so I cannot match him step by step, but I have read and written enough to be able to attack his position effectively, or at least I think so. I certainly want to destroy his arguments.

Singer is a seasoned and powerful debater, however. He expects and prepares for critiques from minds much more acute than mine, and so qualifies and limits his argument somewhat. He would not *require* that disabled infants be killed, but simply wants to establish that it can be morally right to do so. He would only grant the power to make such a difficult decision to the parents, not the government. Given the gravity of the situation, he suggests other factors that might be considered. If the parents were able to have another, typical child, thus replacing the worldly pain associated with the disabled infant, then this would work in favor of killing the latter. If the resources devoted to caring for the disabled child reduced the chances of happiness for other, typical children, this would weigh in favor of death for the disabled. And killing would be further justified if the disabled child brought pain and suffering, unrequited by any sort of unexpected happiness, to his parents and siblings. Singer assumes that all of these conditions will obtain.

"Daddy, what's a seizure like?"

One night Margaret, then five, asked me this question, gazing up from the safety and comfort of her bed. It was past eight o'clock and she should have been sleeping but she was worried for Aidan, asleep in his bed beside hers. She had heard him snoring, which sounded like some of his convulsions, and called me into the room: "Daddy, Aidan's having seizures." Fortunately, it was just a snore that night. I reassured her that he was safe but she wanted to know more; she wanted to know what seizures were like, to have a better understanding of her brother's experience.

"Seizures are like..."

I began to answer her question, struggling to find words to explain the complexities of pediatric neurology to a five-year-old.

"They come in different ways. Sometimes Aidan shakes all over—you've seen that before—well, that's a seizure. Sometimes he stretches out his arms and legs and laughs out loud. That's also a kind of seizure. And sometimes his body just jerks once very quickly: that's another type of seizure."

"Does it hurt?" she asked.

"Most of the time it doesn't."

The concern slowly melted from her face as she snuggled her favorite stuffed dog. I kissed her forehead and said good night again. As I left the room and lingered in the hall-way for a moment, I heard her quietly talking to Aidan. Her words were too muffled for me to distinguish, but it was the sound of close and loving talk between siblings, even if Aidan was mute. For Margaret, his silence did not hinder the conversation.

Her love for him has always been uncomplicated. He has been a constant element in her calculations of happiness.

On her fourth Christmas, she began to ask Santa to bring specific presents. Her primary request was a Barbie doll, the African-American mermaid Barbie in particular. She had seen this in a department store and was captivated by the sparkly gold swim suit and the long flowing black hair. But she was also aware that Aidan could not tell us what he wanted; she knew he could not express his desires in the language she was mastering so quickly. So, she did it for him.

"Aidan wants a mermaid Barbie, too. The blond one."

My wife and I, when we were alone together later, laughed out loud at her apparent ploy. She seemed to be using him to procure a second doll for herself. How wily for a four-year-old! But the more I pondered it, the more I realized that she was genuinely well-intentioned. Barbie, to her, was the embodiment of fun and beauty, and that was what she believed Aidan would want if he could only tell us. It was obvious to her that he deserved at least the same good fortune as she. After Santa dutifully brought the two dolls, Margaret carefully eased the blond mermaid into the cushion of Aidan's wheelchair and happily invented a play world for them all. She politely let him know if she took the blond mermaid elsewhere, maybe into the tub with her, but it was known for some time as Aidan's Barbie. Margaret made sure of that.

There are myriad other ways in which Margaret has looked after her brother. Sometimes she has suddenly and clearly seen something that Aidan would like and acted on her discoveries enthusiastically.

One evening, Aidan was resting in his bed as Maureen and Margaret and I were about to begin our dinner. Although we often have him with us in the kitchen or dining room, this evening he was obviously tired and needed to be stretched out in bed. Fish was our main course and we had some lemon juice on the table in a bumpy, rounded little vessel that was supposed to resemble the sour fruit. With a flash of inspiration, Margaret seized the yellow plastic receptacle and dashed down the hallway. We called after her:

"What are you doing?"

"I'm taking the lemon to Aidan so he can feel it."

She knew the ridged surface would be a novel tactile experience for him. She literally jumped to bring a little piece of the world to her sightless and speechless brother.

However discomforting Singer's kill-the-baby arguments may be, they are exceptional only in their brutal directness. In fact, the underlying devaluation of disabled life is very widespread in American society, in most societies. While many people would probably not support infanticide, not publicly at least, they might find themselves agreeing that it would have been "better" if Aidan had died on any of the several occasions when death was near. When happiness is presumably outweighed by pain, death seems, to many, better than disability.

We have encountered this sad calculation in various forms. Once, just after a bad bout of pneumonia when Aidan was three and Margaret one, a visiting nurse was assigned to help us manage his care at home. She was a chatty and energetic person, rushing about from one patient's house to another, bringing skilled care and a little gossip when she came. Maureen knew her from the hospital, where their paths had crossed a couple of years before, and trusted her as a nurse and confidante. She was fiercely loyal to Aidan, willing to battle with bureaucrats of various stripes to get him what he needed. We welcomed her feisty interventions. During one of her visits, she mentioned to us an exchange she had had with an insurance company functionary. She was making the case for additional services for Aidan. The company did not want the extra expense. They went back and forth until the testy technocratic voice on the other end of the telephone blurted out a telling accusation:

"It's all their fault, the parents, for keeping these kinds of kids alive..."

Keeping him alive: yes, we were guilty as charged. Before the worst *status epilepticus*, if we had drawn up a stricter code procedure, one that denied all forms of resuscitation, maybe he would have died. If we had not acceded to the feeding tube, perhaps the pneumonias would have eventually killed him. If Maureen had been a little slower in responding on the tenth day of his life, the first wave of seizures might have done him in. Yes, we have kept him alive.

So much was said in that one sentence. The bureaucrat was likely staring into some file that showed the great expense of Aidan's care. Many resources had already been spent and his prognosis, from a medical point of view, remained poor. The costs, it appeared, were outstripping the benefits. The insurance company agent had never met Aidan or us, she had no real understanding of our situation. All the spreadsheets she consulted said nothing of the satisfaction we felt when he was settled and comfortable in his own bed, with his loving sister nearby. The numbers could not show his smile. They told only a narrow economic story, devoid of vital context and humanity. It was the same utilitarian logic that Singer used: if the ostensible balance of pain and pleasure, bad and good, cost and benefit, turned up a deficit, you were less than zero, better off dead.

A somewhat less morbid, though still depressingly callous, encounter with the dismal science of the actuaries caught me by surprise about two years later. It was many months after the placement of the g-j tube; we were well into the regimen of intestinal feeding. Everything was going well: Aidan was getting good nourishment; the pneumonias were vanquished; we had learned how to create a routine that was only minimally disruptive to his school day. In fact, what had once seemed like a terrible step back-ward—tube-feeding—was now just another ordinary ele-ment of our daily schedule. While Aidan had lost the sensation of taste, he had gained weight and health. It was not that bad at all.

Then the letter came. The HMO had been covering the full cost of the overpriced formula we needed. Our monthly bill for just his food was over $1,000. Why a 250-milliliter can of not-very-complicated liquid had to cost almost $10 was beyond me, but, with no real alternatives, we had to pay the going price. So, I should not have been too shocked when I opened the envelope from the insurance company. The message stated that after "careful review" it had been decided that the "supplementary nutritional supplies" that "Aiden" was taking were "not medically necessary." There-fore, the company would no longer cover the cost of said "supplementary nutritional supplies." We could appeal the decision through the proper company channels but it was expected that we would assume financial responsibility for the food ourselves or the state welfare agencies would inter-vene. The letter was signed by a woman purporting to be a medical doctor, complete with "M.D." after her name.

I was astonished. It was so patently false, the assertion that Aidan's food was "not medically necessary." It was so remarkable that they suggested a "careful review" had been done—they could not even spell his name correctly! It was so obvious that it was accountants, not doctors, who were pressing to dump this expense from the books.

At first, I did not know where to begin to rebut this feeble attempt to rationalize away my son's sole source of nourishment and primary defense against pulmonary contagion. But I was trained to argue. After absorbing the initial shock, I consulted our contract with the HMO. They were clearly wrong: I could cite them chapter and verse from their own legal documents justifying the provision of tube-feeding supplies. Then, I honed in on the key premise of their fallacious argument, the notion that Aidan's food was somehow "supplemental." This characterization had an extraordinarily absurd feel to it, as if we would have gone through all of the struggle over the g-j tube just to give him a little of this or a pinch of that every once in a while. You know, just after gobbling down a big meal, he could top it off with a glass of soda right into his small intestine. My confidence was rising to the point of enjoyment. It was going to be fun to utterly embarrass these money-clutching bean-counters, to destroy their assertions to the point of their humiliation. I reached for the phone.

When I finally got through to someone who had a role in the company's appeals process, I unloaded on him. Did they know that we were talking about my son's only source of sustenance? Did they know about the pneumonias? Had they bothered to talk to us, his parents, or his primary care physician, or the long list of specialists who had actually seen him over the years? Had they read the contract they had sent me? And, of course, did they know I had contacted my lawyer? I hadn't, really, but, what the heck, I was on a roll. The young man on the other end of the line listened intently. I could almost hear his face tighten up as he gradually realized that they had blown it. He would look into it, he said, and get back to me as soon as he could. I told him I would copy my lawyer on the letter I was sending in reply to the "doctor" who had dared sign this sorry excuse for a "careful review."

I wrote the letter, but did not copy it to a lawyer. The young man called back the next day, apologetic and helpful. He couched his response in administrative niceties that meant nothing to me. I knew I had won this skirmish. The insurance company would continue to pay for the formula, at least until they could find some other way out of it.

The warmth of victory did not last, however. As I contemplated the whole affair, I saw it as representative of the broader domination of utilitarian thinking. Aidan was costly, his care was using up finite resources that might have gone to some other good purpose. For what the company spent on him, several other cases might be supported. The greatest good for the greatest number could arguably be better served by cutting off Aidan. This happened all the time, I was sure. Both private and public institutions responsible for caring for people, disabled or not, routinely tried to cut their case loads. The insurance companies were searching for profit, while state agencies were hopelessly under-funded and unable to fulfill their missions. Whatever the remote cause, the effect was the same: cost-cutting and efficiency were the watchwords of the day. In this competitive milieu, each dollar had to be made to go farther, money could not be wasted on just one profoundly mentally retarded boy who would never walk or talk or see anyway. *It's all their fault, the parents, for keeping these kinds of kids alive...*

The insurance company might have won their not-medically-necessary argument had I not fought back spiritedly. If I were less assertive or less comfortable with the language or just scared of the system, they would have stopped paying for the food, pushing the responsibility onto us or the state welfare system—even though they were contractually obligated. Clearly, they were not inhibited by any higher principle, legal or otherwise. We had, after all, been paying our premiums regularly. They were simply pressing for their financial advantage and I was able to marshal enough resistance to make them back down. I had prevailed this time, but I might not the next. Such is the plight of the few, the minority, in any utilitarian world. We are the ones who are supposed to sacrifice, or be sacrificed, in the name of a greater good that does not include us.

The saddest thing of all was the "doctor" who had signed the letter. She passed judgment on Aidan's case without ever examining him or consulting his primary pediatrician or speaking to us. And her decision was significant for what it said: his formula was supplementary and medically unnecessary. The gastroenterologists who had placed the g-j tube would have been surprised by these assertions, put forth, as they were, without the slightest shred of supporting evidence. The letter-writing doctor was, to my mind, not really a doctor at all, but a businesswoman in a white coat, looking to spruce up the bottom line, maybe pull down a bonus for cutting costs. And in seeking her pay in this manner, she was effectively violating her professional oath. She was not acting in the best interest of the patient. That is what money can do, especially when its role is obscured by specious argumentation.

It's not just money that distorts our view of human worth. Social status, cultural attainment, physical beauty: all of these and more creep into our calculations of an individual's value. These sorts of criteria are so commonplace that it sometimes seems remarkable when we are reminded that none of them fully capture the possibilities of personhood. And that is what Aidan does.

His value comes precisely from the challenge he poses to the usual definitions of "value." He is a living reminder that the range of human experience is broader than the narrow confines of balance sheets and business plans. Without a word, he poses the deepest questions. What is a life? What makes any life, even one so limited, worth it? Strangers have come up to us on crowded streets, touching his shoulder or tousling his hair, giving us their abbreviated answers. Usually they say something about love or grace, something well beyond the material concerns of everyday life. We are constantly reminded of these more sublime things because, with

Aidan, it's never about utility or efficiency or productivity, it's about humanity.

For Chuang Tzu, rationality is what makes us human. Yet, unlike Singer, he sees this not as a reason for privileged ethical status, but as a cause of our sadness. Our analytic capacities distinguish us from other animals and the natural milieu, but it is precisely that alienation from nature that clouds our vision of Way, the vast expanse of all things complete unto themselves and all together.

An ancient Chinese logician once asked Chuang Tzu if it was possible for a person to have no nature. Chuang Tzu replied, yes, that was possible and the logician pressed on to inquire how one could be called human if he had no nature. Chuang Tzu then said:

Yes this and no that—that's what I call human nature...
Not mangling yourself with good and bad—that's what I
call no nature. Instead of struggling to improve on life,
you simply abide in occurrence appearing of itself.

The logician responded:

If you don't try to improve on life, how do you stay alive?

And Chuang Tzu answered:

Tao gives you shape and heaven gives you form, so why mangle yourself with good and bad?

Each thing is what it is. The distinctions we create in our minds—*yes this and no that*—have no bearing on the fullness and movement of the Way. It is futile to try to determine who should live and who should die. We will all die. Whether a life is deemed good or bad matters not in the end, when our bodily forms give way.

Chuang Tzu is not a nihilist; there is a right and a wrong for him. His morality, however, eschews man-made analytic categories. It rests, rather, in the rightness of not upsetting the natural course of events. It is, of course, difficult to know the "natural course of events," but even with this uncertainty, some principles emerge. To kill another human being is bad, for that would be taking away the shape given by Tao and the form given by heaven. Indeed, any sort of harm to others is likely to be, in Chuang Tzu's eyes, a wrongful act. He wants us to respect each thing in the world for what it is in itself. His is an ethic of tolerance, deference, and humility.

On the other hand, in our efforts to stave off Aidan's death, have we violated these principles? Have we gone too far to improve on his life? Not really, I think. We have to gauge what is appropriate and necessary based upon the particular qualities of each individual. Proper medical interventions for Aidan will be determined by who he is in himself, his shape and form. The feeding tube, which might appear as the epitome of the unnatural to some people, is, for him, a straightforward extension of his condition. The VNS, a high-tech gadget, is not as unusual as it might seem to the uninitiated. It is practically homeopathic, following the precept of herbal practitioners of using minute amounts of substances to induce effects similar to the disease process itself—using like things to treat like problems—it creates an insubstantial pulse of electricity to counter the phantom of seizures. No, we have not gone too far, but we have gone far enough to know when medical treatment for Aidan should stop. We have signed the letter detailing for doctors and emergency technicians precisely what *not* to do if his heart should stop beating. We have some sense of when to *abide in occurrence appearing of itself.*

In trying to draw such fine lines between life and death, however, we are drifting back to the strict rationality that cuts us off from a fuller appreciation of the complexity of life. We are, like Singer, relying on our rationalistic human nature instead of accepting *no nature.* Maybe, as humans, there is no complete escape from this predicament. Instead, we must be humble in the face of the enormity of the Way and not elevate ourselves too grandly. As Chuang Tzu observes elsewhere:

People think we're different from baby birds cheeping,
but are we saying any more than they are?

We do not banter, Aidan and I. There is no verbal jousting, the child exercising mind and language in a match of wits against the parent. Margaret, by contrast, is quick to express herself, to hold me to my words, to make a joke. Aidan is unspeaking. His sounds certainly tell us when he is tired or hurting or happy. But our intellectual exchanges are based largely on his silence.

He inspires silence in me. When I walk into his room, I do not want to speak, but, rather, absorb the surroundings as he does, radiate my presence to him without words. This is not a good impulse, however. All the therapists tell us that we must engage him orally to alert him to our approach, to avoid startles and disorientation. Maureen is exceptionally good at this, always announcing her comings and goings to him in clear voice. I have to fight back against Aidan's still-ing effect. I want to follow him into his quiet, but I ought to bring him into the world of the talking, they say.

Since he has no conventional voice of his own, we find ourselves speaking for him, narrating his life to the world. We do this every day in the immediate ambit of his activities. I tell Maureen that he has had a seizure, or that he seems tired, or whatever it is that I see in him. She tells me what she perceives about him. We tell his school aide how his morning went. We tell the insurance companies that he is human. This is not just a one-way street. We represent him to other people, and then give back to him our translations of what is out there beyond his senses. It is a dynamic exchange of information.

For myself, I have found that I can write his life as well as speak it. And this has enlarged his imprint on the world.

It started out rather modestly. Late one summer, when he was six years old, I noticed that a small magazine of Catholic social thought, *Commonweal*, ran human interest stories on their back page. Short profiles of individuals facing some sort of personal crisis seemed common. I started to write about Aidan with this page in mind. I described his condition, and mentioned his effect on me and on his classmates at school. Not used to non-academic writing and publishing, I did not know what to expect when I submitted it, unsolicited, to the editor. It hardly mattered what I thought, however, because they quickly accepted it and published it later that fall, three weeks before his seventh birthday.

This spurred me on. The next spring, I wrote another short piece, one that sharply rejected using any notion of "productivity" to measure Aidan's worth. Setting my sights higher, I sent it to the Sunday magazines of several high-profile national newspapers: the *Washington Post*, the *New York Times*, the *Los Angeles Times*. I waited. Nothing happened. It turned out that these journals received so many unsolicited manuscripts that they could not even acknowledge receipt of them. As spring turned to summer and summer turned to fall, I did not know what to do with the article. Frustrated, I sent it to the opinion page of the *New York Times*, fully expecting another rejection. My fax went in on a Sunday afternoon; they replied the next morning. They wanted it. The op-ed editor must have been sitting in her office on that same Sunday and seen the piece as it crossed her desk. Aidan had captured her attention.

Things moved along fairly quickly, and about two weeks later the piece ran, right next to fellow Singapore-basher William Safire's biweekly column. And with that, Aidan was momentarily cast into a national spotlight.

Letters and emails poured in from around the country. Parents of disabled children wrote back with their stories. Alumni of my college corresponded with their thoughts. A woman from Greece emailed with questions about Aidan's diagnosis and how it compared with her son's condition. Perhaps most remarkable was a ninth-grade English teacher from Murray Bergtraum High School in Manhattan. She cut out the article and gave it to her students to read and discuss. With her note to me she sent along twenty other letters written by her class. They reflected upon Aidan and his place in the world. I read them all to Aidan, becoming the moderator of a long-distance conversation. From his bedroom in Massachusetts, Aidan was connected with a new band of fiercely loyal friends and, beyond that, people all around who had stopped and centered him in their minds for a time.

I write his life for others and, through these stories, find new life for myself.

In following Aidan, I had wandered into the civic activism of the PAC, and, as time went on, the path of public service expanded for me. As I began my third year chairing the PAC, a position opened up on the School Committee, the town's elected body that oversees policies and finances for public education. Aidan was six, not yet in kindergarten; Margaret was three, still at home with Maureen. I was safely tenured in my teaching job. The terrible time of the kidney stones had not yet happened. Our lives seemed fairly manageable. So, we could contemplate a spot on the School Committee.

Maureen thought she might like to do it. She went to one of the monthly meetings, however, and came home discouraged. That night a crowd of people had come with complaints about the firing of a bus driver. It was an uncharacteristically tumultuous meeting, with people shouting and hurling insults (usually hardly anyone attended). Maureen was put off. She could not see herself patiently listening to overwrought parents grumble about trivial problems. So she said I should do it.

It was not that I was especially good at listening. Rather, Maureen thought that someone with background in disability issues and special education needed to be on the School Committee. At that point, none of the current members appeared to have much experience in the area. After a little over two years on the PAC, I had some familiarity with how disabled kids fared in the school. Also, the administration had just hired an outside consultant to evaluate the special education program and make recommendations for improvements. The PAC had been involved with this effort, and I was interested to see how the School Committee would follow through on it. Taking up a position at this moment might allow me to have a part in making the school more inclusive and effective. The time seemed right.

We were also thinking more directly about Aidan. Administrators, teachers, and staff members would likely pay more attention to him and his program if his father was on the School Committee. This may have been self-serving but, after years of struggling to make sure he got some of what he needed in school, and never being confident about the treatment of disabled children, we felt we had to defend his interests better.

After thinking it over for some weeks, I finally put my name forward as a candidate. It was a fairly painless process. The open seat was to be filled by appointment for the remainder of the year. I would have to run for election the following spring. But smalltown politics being what they were, there were no other contenders for the position. So, as we rounded the new year, I said good-bye to the mothers of the PAC and assumed a seat on the School Committee, where I would remain for the next four and a half years.

It took some time to get a feel for the work. That first half year was easy enough: I just sat and said little at our monthly meetings, watching and listening to the flow of business. We met in a modest third floor conference room at the school, five of us arrayed behind a table at one end of the room, plus the superintendent and the principal at opposite ends of our row. Twenty feet in front of us were forty or so chairs for any interested onlookers, usually only two or three civic-minded souls. Fluorescent lights bathed all in a stark white glow. At the back of the room a video camera blinked, broadcasting our meetings on the local-access cable channel.

Our agenda was full. The budget was complicated, the teacher's contract contentious, and the emerging requirements of standardized testing unwelcome. Special Education was just one rather small part of this world.

At the end of the school year I made an impassioned plea for a summer program better adapted to the needs of the disabled children, but the money wasn't there, nor was the staffing, so nothing happened. We did, however, vote unanimously to create a new staff position: an "inclusion facilitator," a person to take charge of the most severely disabled children and coordinate their services to make sure they were effectively integrated into the regular classrooms. The consultant had recommended this idea; it seemed like a step forward.

I came to see, however, that there were larger issues that dominated both special and regular education. Chief among these was tax revenue for our budget. In Massachusetts, as in so many states, the primary source of money for education comes from local property taxes. The state government will contribute some funds from its general income tax receipts, but most of our money was drawn from householders and landlords in our town. There was a state law, moreover, that limited any annual increase in the local property tax rate to no more than 2 1/2 percent. This meant that school spending was strictly limited. Any budget increase beyond 2 1/2 percent had to come out of other town services or increased state aid. If those options were not available, some school activities had to be cut or a referendum had to be held to override the 2 1/2 percent tax cap.

The reliance on limited property tax revenue created a debilitating struggle for money within both the school and the town. With funds so limited, expensive special education costs, like paying for Aidan's aide and his physical therapy sessions, were essentially competing against expenditures for regular education. But federal law—the Individuals with Disabilities Education Act—mandated that special education services *had* to be provided regardless of cost. So, when the budget was tight, parents of typical children would protest that their kids were getting short shrift. These frustrations were usually not publicly aired because parents did not want to be labeled as insensitive toward the disabled, but tension was never far from the surface of certain conversations. The stern PAC mother became a convenient scapegoat for a financing scheme well beyond her control.

The best solution, it seemed to me, was to avoid competition between special education and regular education. Since a significant portion of Aidan's needs shaded off into the medical realm, as opposed to being strictly educational, it would make a good deal of sense to pay for some of these activities through a broader statewide program, which would take the burden off local taxpayers. A reordering of priorities at the state level could easily finance new public policies for the disabled. I wrote op-ed pieces in the county newspaper, arguing that Boston was shirking its responsibility to disabled children, and effectively weakening its commitment to education. Unsurprisingly, I had no effect in the capital. So, the second best alternative was to organize a local political movement to override the local property tax limit.

Getting people to pay higher taxes is not an easy political objective, even in a college town where a good number of voters strongly support education. In the early 1990s, two tax overrides had been turned down in my town. Those who felt they could not absorb a tax increase turned out at the polls faithfully to defeat any override, even though their own children would stand to gain from good education. They just could not afford it. This bloc was so formidable that the selectmen, the small town New England equivalent of a town council, would not take the lead in pushing for the tax increase. Four years earlier, an override had been defeated and the elementary school had to cut its French program. This time, five teaching positions were on the block, likely the end of the music and art curriculum.

I found myself among a group of worried parents, perhaps ten of us in all. None of the others had children in special education. We were not enamored of higher taxes, but saw no other way to preserve our children's education. The school budget was not larded with excessive spending, teachers were not overpaid; any reduction in expenditures would come at the expense of real teaching and learning. We started meeting and planning, working to find a winning electoral strategy. One of my neighbors had worked on referendums when he lived in California, and he had a good sense of what needed to be done. We drafted him to chair our fledgling political action committee and I took up the post of treasurer, responsible for raising money and filing various legal documents with state authorities.

This put me squarely in the middle of the most divisive local politics. It was not China or the prime minister of Singapore, but it was exhilarating. We assembled about sixty campaign workers who together systematically canvassed the town, calling as many homes as possible to identify supporters. If we encountered persuadable skeptics, we worked through the arguments in favor of the tax increase: good schools were central to a healthy town, edifying the children and elevating the community. When we happened upon staunch opponents, we politely closed the conversation. The point was not to enrage our adversaries but just locate our adherents. We wrote everything down, cross-tabulated all the information, and eventually produced long lists of addresses and phone numbers of people who said they would vote for the school tax.

On election day, we took nothing for granted. From a house across the street from the polling place in the elementary school, we called supporters and urged them to get out to vote. Since the record of who had already cast a ballot was public information, we stationed observers as close as legally possible to the voting booths so we could monitor exactly how many backers had voted and when. All afternoon we kept on phoning, offering people rides to the polls, organizing babysitters, getting the message out—anything, everything we could think of to make sure the school would get its funding.

At eight o'clock that evening, when the polls closed, a dozen of us, the most active of the activists, crowded around the town clerk as she jotted down results from the three small voting machines. We knew how many people had voted and we knew how many we needed to win. If half of the roughly four thousand registered voters turned out, eleven hundred would secure a comfortable victory. That was what we were shooting for. The clerk quickly tallied the figures and reminded us that she would have to add the absentee ballots later—only about forty votes. We watched anxiously as she tacked a small sheet of paper with penciled handwriting on a bulletin board by the main door: *for*— 1,426; *against*—1,030. We had won.

The victory not only saved the school budget, it had transformed town politics. Where conventional local wisdom had suggested that overrides were doomed to failure, we had shown how concerted effort could win. Some of the selectmen marveled at our strategy and methods. They had never seen anything quite like it. We had made some enemies—an inevitability of political action—but we had eased the strain within the school between special and regular education. It was worth the fight.

Later, at a celebratory party full of happy and boisterous campaigners and supporters, I thought of Aidan. He had propelled me into this moment. Whatever positive effect I had helped to create—from recruiting my politically savvy neighbor to managing campaign finances to rallying supporters— all was generated by him. By getting on the School Committee,

I thought I would be helping him, but he had had a greater impact on me. He had led me into the PAC, which pointed me toward the School Committee, which catapulted me into this campaign and this victory. Without doing anything directly by himself, he had left nothing undone.

And there was more.

While the override campaign was unfolding, I had been appointed as the School Committee's representative to a town working group charged with exploring whether we needed a new elementary school building. It seemed obvious to me that something drastic needed to be done. One section of the decrepit structure was literally a hundred years old and showing its age. Tight budgets for many years—before our most recent victory—had left the town unable to maintain the facility adequately. The chipped bricks, sagging boilers, and leaky roof were testaments to the shortcomings of public finance. Most bothersome to me was the fact that Aidan could not gain access to the upper floor of one wing for lack of an elevator. As a result, he could not even be considered for placement into the classrooms of some of the best kindergarten teachers.

As it turned out, I was not alone in my impression of the building's deficiencies. Our working group, which included the school superintendent and the town manager and a selectman, hired an architect to come and analyze the structure. His report was devastating: the edifice was stunningly inefficient, embarrassingly obsolete, and in need of many costly repairs and improvements. We passed this information on to another, larger committee, to which I was also appointed, which quickly came to the conclusion that the best course of action was construction of a new school. This would mean another political campaign to obtain public support and financing.

So, one year after the successful tax override vote, we were at it again, gearing up our political machine to convince people to authorize a new school. We were fairly confident this time around, even though the financial goal was much higher: a bond issue to cover a $14.5 million project. We knew where to start and what to do. More people, different people got involved and took on leadership positions. The message slowly spread, rousing the interest of more and more residents. Through strategy sessions and public meetings and mass mailings, the momentum of the campaign grew.

The crucial moment came at a special town meeting. This was a traditional New England political institution. Each year all registered voters were called into the gymnasium of the elementary school to decide major town business. All budgets had to be approved by majority vote; any changes in zoning laws needed to pass the scrutiny of town meeting; all important policy initiatives had to come before this gathering of the people. But this was a special town meeting, still with all its legislative authority but called to consider only the question of the new school. A two-thirds majority of the voting members present was required to approve the bond issue.

For a typical town meeting, a turnout of four to five hundred people, perhaps just above 10 percent of all registered voters, was standard. This November night was obviously different, however. I arrived early, to huddle with my comrades and plan how we would respond to any questions that might come from the crowd. As the time neared for the opening gavel, the cavernous gym was packed with people. The bleachers were full; all the chairs on the floor were taken; people stood against the walls and in the doorways. Old timers said they had never seen so many people at a town meeting. But were they our supporters or our adversaries?

The lead advocate for the new school made a short presentation and then opened the floor for questions. We had anticipated certain queries and decided which topic each of us should take. I had recently been elevated to chair of the School Committee, one of the dozen or so most important leadership positions in town, and I was responsible for any questions on how the new building would affect our budget or other policies. At one point, about ten minutes into the proceedings, someone rose and asked if we would save money on maintenance costs in the new school. I got up from my seat in the front row, turned and faced the throng and reassured the questioner that, yes, we anticipated savings in our maintenance budget. The air in the rustling hall was hot and thick.

A few minutes later, a member of the audience yelled out, "Call the question."

By parliamentary rules, which we followed, this meant that a vote had to be taken immediately to determine whether debate should be ended. The moderator dutifully discharged this task, and by an overwhelming voice vote, the meeting decided to cut off debate and move directly to a vote to approve or disapprove the new school bond issue. The moment had arrived. For me, it was more than a year's worth of committee meetings and planning sessions and telephone conferences, all reduced to the few seconds it would take for the majority to utter its judgment.

The moderator called out, "All those in favor, please say, Aye."

A thunderous roar of *ayes* rained down from every direction.

"All those opposed, please say, Nay."

A thin, almost inaudible sigh of *nays* whispered through the immense room.

It was Aidan, again. He had brought me here. Whatever role I had played was as an agent of his existence.

About a year and a half later, ground was broken for the new school building. Every time I passed the site, and watched the workmen scramble up their scaffolds to place their bricks and trowel their mortar, I saw a concrete expression of Aidan's effect on the world.

Peter Singer could not kill his mother.

It turned out that she contracted Alzheimer's disease and descended into irrationality. She was, by the dictates of her son's system of ethics, no longer a person. Were he to remain faithful to his philosophy, he would not expend money and medical resources on her care; he would not try to prolong her life; he might even work actively to bring about her demise. But he could not do it. Instead, he spent his own funds, earned from his famous philosophizing, for her home health-care aides. He kept her alive.

Writers and journalists questioned him about his apparent inability to live up to his own rigorously argued criteria for an ethical life. To the *New Yorker*, he replied: "I think this has made me see how the issues of someone with these kinds of problems are really very difficult. Perhaps it is more difficult than I thought before, because it is different when it's your mother."

He did not rescind his basic line of reasoning, however. Indeed, after the revelation of his mother's condition, he reissued key passages of his rationale for infanticide and euthanasia in a new collection of his work. Another journal, *Reason* magazine, reported that "he is not the only person who is involved in making decisions about his mother (he has a sister). He did say that if he were solely responsible, his mother might not be alive today."

But he didn't do it. Either his love for his mother or his respect for his sister stilled the killing logic. In either case, blood proved thicker than utilitarianism.

People think we're different from baby birds cheeping,
but are we saying any more than they are?

One of Chuang Tzu's most potent metaphors is the useless tree. He marks its significance by invoking it, directly or indirectly, at least five different times in the early chapters of his book. The central image is a gigantic tree, gnarled and knotty, with rotting wood and fetid leaves. It is apparently worthless, devoid of alluring fruit or durable timber. Attracting little attention, it has grown unencumbered, spreading out its branches so that *it could shelter a thousand teams of horses in its shade.* It stands in silent denial of our obsessions with the useful, the productive, the efficient, the worthy.

Chuang Tzu draws at least three interrelated messages from this image.

If you have no use, you have no grief.

This first interpretation points to liberation. Without the appeal of utility, the tree is not cut down; it grows to mammoth proportions while those with sweet fruit or beautiful wood are hacked and cut until, wounded, they die. It is the classic Taoist idea: by doing nothing, the useless tree gains what we all seek. It escapes death and grief.

From this perspective, Aidan has certain advantages. Although he is not liberated from the pains and inflictions of his body, he is spared the man-made sorrows that can crash down upon us. He did not watch those proud New York towers crumble in flame and ash, casting a palpable wave of sadness that reached all the way up to our little corner of Massachusetts—we could feel Staten Island crying. He does not have to struggle, as Margaret now does, with my rudimentary explanations of war and terrorism and suicide. Some people are consumed, either as perpetrators or victims or hapless spectators, by the more banal evils that fill too much of our experience. But such things hardly ever impinge upon Aidan's consciousness. He does not see or feel malevolence. There is much he misses of the world, but, at the same time, there is a certain peace in his life.

A second reading of the useless tree points to other possibilities:

> Everyone knows that to be useful is useful, but who knows how useful it is to be useless?

Here there is a suggestion of inadvertent accomplishment. Utility can be found in the apparently useless tree. In one version of the story the ugly behemoth stands next to, and shelters, the village shrine, becoming, through its impressive immensity, a part of the shrine itself. It has a certain function. In another rendition, Chuang Tzu says that the good-for-nothing hulk is, actually, good precisely for its provision of nothingness:

> Why not plant it in a village where there's nothing at all, a land where emptiness stretches away forever! Then, you could be no one drifting lazily beside it, roam boundless and free as you doze in its shade.

The tree thus becomes a facilitator, bringing those who care to use it closer to the Way.

I often find myself thinking of Aidan in these terms. He obviously has a powerful effect on me and Maureen and his sister, and on his classmates and on so many who come in contact with him. My life has been transformed. I have come to see that it matters little whether I characterize the change as "good" or "bad." Rather, it is the awareness of change itself—and how other changes will come and push me along—that is his greatest gift to me. Not too long ago, I understood myself as a student of Chinese politics, a detached and dispassionate analyst, but then I became a local politician myself, immersed and committed to particular outcomes. Never would I have imagined such a turnabout in my life; never, that is, before Aidan. Now, anything seems possible.

Sometimes I push this line of thinking further, in a direction Chuang Tzu would likely resist, to justify Aidan's existence against the onslaught of the insurance companies and accountants and other champions of productivity and utility. I can say that many of the changes Aidan has wrought in my life are good, and those goods might never have existed had he not been who he is. So, when calculating the value of Aidan's life, as the utilitarians are wont to do, these other effects, which so often escape view because of their indirectness, must also be added in. There are many ways, some unseen, that he matters.

But Chuang Tzu finds another nuance in the useless tree, one that stops me in my tracks when I am contemplating Aidan's life:

Look, it isn't like the rest of us: it's harboring something
utterly different. If we praise its practicality, we'll miss
the point altogether, won't we?

There is no need for calculation and assessment. All of these are merely vain attempts to make sense of his life in terms of my own able-bodied comprehension. But if each thing is integral unto itself; if *...the real is originally there in things, and the sufficient is originally there in things. There's nothing that is not real and nothing that is not sufficient...* then, why should I ever worry about the meaning of his life? *It is! It just is!* Perhaps it would be better to reverse field and try to understand myself, or at least my place in the Way, in terms of his atypical experience. Or maybe it would be best to not even try to understand, in some formal rational way, but just see. Otherwise...

...we'll miss the point altogether, won't we?

Bibliographic Note

Learning about your child's disabled brain is a daunting task. My first reference was an old, out-of-date textbook that Maureen had brought home from the hospital and had planned to ship off to the nursing school in China where she had worked. It was a thick book with short chapters on a host of brain malformations. The pictures were bizarre and depressing. It was here I discovered the rudiments of agenesis of the corpus callosum, polymicrogyria and the like. A more recent scientific source is *Congenital Malformations of the Brain* by Margaret G. Norman (Oxford, 1995). As a counterpoint, a good overview of typical early child development written for the general reader is Laura E. Berk's *Infants and Children* (Allyn and Bacon, 2001). For understanding seizures, a book that has been very helpful to us is: *Seizures and Epilepsy in Childhood* John M. Freeman, et al. (Johns Hopkins, 1990).

Internet-based materials on disabilities are plentiful and useful. A good starting point is the site of the National Organization for Rare Disorders (NORD): *www.rarediseases.org*. They maintain a database on a wide range of diagnoses and conditions, with links to relevant organizations. One such group is the Agenesis of the Corpus Callosum (ACC) Network, a small operation run by the parents of a young man with ACC, now based at the University of Maine at Orono. I have drawn on some of their material for illustration of this condition. They do not have a website, but can be reached via email (*um-acc@maine.maine.edu*). Another good portal into web resources is the National Institutes of Health—*www.nih.gov*—and, for neurological issues, the National Institute of Neurological Disorders and Stroke (NINDS): *www.ninds.nih.gov*. One university site that informed my descriptions of brain development is the Virtual Hospital at the University of Iowa: *www.vh.org*, especially Adel K. Afifi and Ronald A. Bergman's text, "The Fetal and Young Child Nervous System: The Story of the Development and Maldevelopment of the Brain."

For help in parenting a disabled child, the first place to go is the magazine *Exceptional Parent*. This monthly publication provides a regular stream of information on particular conditions, on special education issues, on medical equipment, and legal and financial matters. The magazine's website—*www.eparent.com*—has many useful links. The greatest solace, we have found, often comes from people facing similar situations; they can be found through the dozens and dozens of support organizations listed in the magazine and on the website.

There are many translations of the Taoist classics. I have drawn on many of them, some more than others.

For the *Book of Changes* (sometimes transliterated as the *I Ching*) I find the Richard Wilhelm/Cary Baynes edition (Princeton, 1967) still the most pleasant translation to read, and I have quoted it in chapters two and six. It is a good starting point for anyone interested in this elusive text. Richard John Lynn's version (Columbia, 1994) is full and erudite, including the politically oriented commentaries of a third-century scholar-official, Wang Pi. Edward Shaughnessy has produced an exceedingly spare, but historically enlightening, rendition (Ballantine, 1997).

The *Tao Te Ching*, attributed to Lao Tzu, has inspired countless translations. I have drawn most heavily on David Hinton's recent edition (Counterpoint, 2000). He is a poet by training and instinct and does a marvelous job bringing out the beauty of the words. All of my direct quotations from the *Tao Te Ching* are taken from Hinton, with permission, unless otherwise noted. I have also used Robert Hendricks's translation (Ballantine, 1989), which works from one of the oldest known original texts. This is the book my father gave me. It is Hendricks's image of the Way as an uncultivated field I cite in chapter two; and it is his translations that I quote on pages XXX, XXX, and XXX. An older version by Lin Yutang (Modern Library, 1948) is the source of the quote on stillness on page XXX. This book is helpful, too, because it relates sections of the *Tao Te Ching* to similar passages in Chuang Tzu's writings.

There are fewer translations of Chuang Tzu. Again, David Hinton has produced perhaps the most eloquent rendering (Counterpoint, 1997). His work is the source of all quotes from Chuang Tzu in this book, used here with permission. I have consulted two other versions, though I have not quoted them: the widely used Burton Watson translation (Columbia, 1968) and the informative volume by A.C. Graham (Mandala, 1991).

Acknowledgments

Writing a book is never a solitary enterprise. Even when tapping away at the keyboard late at night by myself, I was acutely aware of the many people who made possible the conception and execution of this volume.

First of all, my family is my sustenance and my inspiration. Our parents and extended family have lovingly sustained us. Maureen accepted my decision to write our story and helped me remember things she sometimes did not want to remember. Margaret cheerfully recognized that my apparent obsession with the computer as just another facet of our odd normality. And Aidan has changed my life in myriad ways. Whatever is valuable and good in the preceding pages is his doing. He has made me into a writer.

There are dozens and dozens of people—teachers and doctors and nurses and therapists and friends and colleagues—who have helped us over the years and influenced our story. Aidan's life has gained immeasurably from them in large and small ways. They are the social reflection of who he is. To avoid any unintended distractions of their professional practices, I have changed the names of most of the medical practitioners in the text. There are many more people, however, who are not mentioned. It is impossible to thank them all individually; so, a plenary appreciation here will have to do. You know who you are, we know what you have done, and we want you to know that we could not have done it without you.

As for the particulars of the book itself, Dorian Karchmar, my agent, believed in the project from the very beginning, and has worked exceptionally hard with me and for me to see this through to publication. I have learned much from her. Alex Lubertozzi, my editor, has carefully corrected my errors and helped shape the final form of this volume. My thanks to him and all the people at Sourcebooks.

About the Author

Sam Crane is the chair of the Department of Asian Studies, at Williams College; he has written scholarly books and articles as well as numerous articles in the popular press, such as the *New York Times* and *Salon.com* on his son Aidan. He lives in Williamstown, Massachusetts.